ALSO BY

GRETCHEN VON LOEWE KREUTER

An American Dissenter (CO-AUTHOR)

Women of Minnesota (CO-EDITOR)

The Two-Career Family (CO-EDITOR)

Running the Twin Cities

Forgotten Promise

FORGOTTEN PROMISE

Race and Gender Wars on a Small College Campus

A MEMOIR

Gretchen von Loewe Kreuter

Alfred A. Knopf New York 1996

OI BOOK

A. KNOPF, INC.

Published in the United States by Alfred A. Knopf, Inc., New York,
and simultaneously in Canada by Random House of Canada Limited, Toronto.
Distributed by Random House, Inc., New York.

http://www.randomhouse.com/

Library of Congress Cataloging-in-Publication Data

Kreuter, Gretchen von Loewe.
Forgotten promise : race and gender wars on a small college campus /
by Gretchen von Loewe Kreuter.—1st ed.
p. cm.
ISBN 0-679-44700-8
1. Discrimination in higher education—United States—Case studies.
2. Sex discrimination in higher education—United States—Case studies.
3. Minorities—Education (Higher)—United States—Case studies.
4. Women—Education (Higher)—United States—Case studies.
5. Small colleges—United States—Case studies.
I. Title.
LC212.42.K74 1996
370.19'342—dc20 96-25553
CIP

Manufactured in the United States of America
First Edition

For Bob and the Tackies

Acknowledgments

I am deeply indebted to several people who read early drafts of this manuscript and gave me the benefit of their thinking. Among them are Professor Annette Atkins of St. John's University, who did a detailed and sympathetic reading, even though her own personal and professional cares and obligations were substantial; Jane Curry, a recovering academic, who read chapters when they were neither quite essay nor memoir and told me so; and David Kreuter, himself a writer, who helped me sharpen the focus of my memoir, in part by calling my attention to meanings I had not seen in what I had written.

I have discussed parts of this story with several others: including Peg Meier of the Minneapolis *Star Tribune* and Deborah Miller of the Minnesota Historical Society, and I have tried to answer the questions they raised. I have benefited from conversations with Betsy Kreuter Rymes, a doctoral student at UCLA, whose research in applied linguistics centers on discourse and language analysis in urban schools. She would not necessarily agree, I think, with my interpretation of my experiences at Middleton College, or with some of the actions I took, but she helped me look at them from a different perspective.

I was fortunate to have two very different years of conversation and reflection: one as a senior fellow in the Office of Minorities in Higher Education at the American Council on

Education, in Washington, D.C.; the other as an honorary fellow at the Institute for Research in the Humanities at the University of Wisconsin. Hector Garza, director of OMHE/ACE, was a daily reminder of how difficult the task is to increase minority access to higher education. Director Paul Boyer and the fellows of the Humanities Institute helped rekindle my love of the world of intellect and scholarship, even while I was pursuing a much messier project than any of theirs. Their wit and erudition were sustaining influences.

I owe a special debt of gratitude to my husband, Robert L. Sutton, who lived through the events I wrote about, listened to me read sections of this recollection aloud, heard my repetitions of all the "Aha!" moments that came to me as I wrote, and never seemed to find any of it tiresome. "Tell me what you really think," I would insist. "I really think it's wonderful," he would say, and even when I knew it wasn't really, I was glad he said so. Every writer needs one critic like him.

Finally, I am grateful to Jane Garrett of Alfred A. Knopf, who found this project worthy, and helped me make it worthier.

Contents

Preface

This book is a personal memoir of one year I spent as interim president of Middleton College (not its real name), a small midwestern college that attained national attention when it had an incident of racial conflict in 1992.

Originally I planned to write a less intimate account—an extended essay, informed by the Middleton College experience, on race and gender conflict on American campuses today. The essay, as I first conceived it, would include a how-to list for college presidents or Boards of Trustees: how to understand and avoid racial incidents on your campus; how to strengthen the role of minorities on your campus without impairing teaching and learning; how to build a Board of Trustees that reflects the racial and ethnic composition of your college.

As I began to write in that manner, however, I found that my prose either took on the dignified but bloodless quality of a report to a college Board of Trustees or became like many of the useful but dispassionate advisories that appear in journals of higher education. It could have been anybody's essay.

I decided that was not the book I wanted to write. First of all, it would have been presumptuous of me, a white female in late middle age, to write a how-to on minority issues today. Second, such a book would have required me to skim off all the unique richness and flavor of the Middleton experience. It would also have obliged me to tell this story in an attitude of unrelenting seriousness, which is contrary to my nature. Finally, there are very few accounts, written from the perspective of a college president, especially a woman college president, of what it is like to hold such a position in American higher education today. I decided I wanted to write such an account.

Almost immediately, I gained a new respect for memoirists. Opening one's life to the scrutiny and judgment of strangers is not easy. I have taken courage from several women who have written splendid memoirs, but very different from mine: Jill Ker Conway (*The Road from Coorain* and *True North*), Charlayne Hunter-Gault (*In My Place*), Madeleine Kunin (*Living a Political Life*), and Sue Hubbell (*A Country Year*).

I have changed the names of every person and every place connected with the Middleton experience; I have tried to be scrupulously honest in recounting conversations, describing persons and places, and presenting authentically my own thoughts and feelings at any given time. This wasn't easy. The temptation was strong to make a good story better or to caricature instead of characterize. I think I have resisted that temptation.

Much of this memoir is a story of conflict and intolerance. It is worth telling because the Middleton College story shows that there is wisdom and foolishness in every racial, ethnic, or professional group, no matter how well or ill intentioned. It is worth telling because out of the Middleton experience emerge some ideas about how such tensions can be ameliorated, and perhaps even how campuses can move nearer to ideals of justice and equality.

This is a very American story. Nobody any longer believes in some golden age when the melting pot melted, or the tossed salad of nationalities and races mixed happily in the same bowl.

It was never so. Every ethnic, racial, and religious group

has suffered discrimination, has hated and been hated. Today's "model minority"—Asian Americans—were the most despised in times past.

Today, all those groups are now present on our college and university campuses. In earlier times they were found only in the workplace or on the streets of villages and cities. The democratization of American higher education, which is critically important for the continued health and prosperity of the nation and for the attainment of social justice, has brought conflicts onto campuses as never before.

When only privileged young white men attended college, there was much less to quarrel about on campus, and far less likelihood of one person misunderstanding another.

Those days, happily, are gone forever.

When colleges and universities succeed in fulfilling the now-forgotten promise of justice and equality (sometime in the next century) Middleton College will deserve at least a footnote as one of the places where these issues were thrashed out under public scrutiny—where the old campus world met the new head-on, and neither could pretend, any longer, that the other didn't exist.

This is my account of what happened during one critical year of that struggle.

Forgotten Promise

CHAPTER 1

August: Opening Day

Classes began on the last Monday in August at Middleton College. I left my office at 8:30 a.m. to walk around the college quadrangle and get a feel for the occasion and let students become more familiar with who I was, their new interim president. The late-summer sun was bright and warm. A green canopy of oaks and elms shaded the quad, and a high arch of green sheltered the streets. The campus was perfectly groomed, like little children slicked up in their back-to-school outfits. Lawns were cut; flower beds plumped up; evergreens trimmed in the contemporary manner that left no lower branches that might conceal possible assailants. Charlie Fitzgibbon, head of building and grounds, had repainted the Founder's Plaque at my request and had planted red and white impatiens, the college colors, at its base.

The quadrangle was the size of a city block. Across the street on the north side of the quad were the library and the church, both built with native stone. The library was being renovated and expanded, and it wasn't presently in use. Originally, the college had planned to keep the old section open while the new was being constructed, but one day a librarian had noticed a small crack in the common wall between the two. Before her eyes the crack widened; sand and plaster sifted through it. "Everybody out!" she had shouted, and students and staff had rushed out the front door, seconds before the wall collapsed. No one was hurt.

On the east side of the quad was a classroom building, probably built in the 1950s, and behind it was the art building and vehicle maintenance shed. Across the street to the south was a residence hall. (A residence hall, not a dorm. Don't call them dorms, I'd been advised by deans of students on several campuses. Dorms imply just a place to sleep. Residence halls suggest a place where a range of activities takes place, and lots of learning. No doubt about that. Call what happens in them "cocurricular" activities, I was advised, not extracurricular. We must fight the idea that there are two cultures—in classroom and out, curricular and extracurricular. I'd once thought that was a keen educational idea. More recently I'd come to a gloomier conclusion: there weren't two cultures anymore. The cocurricular snake had swallowed the mongoose of learning. On some campuses, little more than a semidigested bulge remained.) Next to the residence halls on another side were two gymnasiums, and, on the other, a music building.

The buildings to the west of the quad were across Main Street, which was really a highway and had been a busy one, too, until recent years when the interstate had diverted most traffic around the village. "Speed Zone Ahead" read the signs at both ends of Middleton, and probably most semis, the ones that still used this route, downshifted as they came through town and campus. Across Main were a dining hall; a combination administration building, women's residence hall, and temporary library; and a too-small parking lot.

All campuses have too-small parking lots. Most church-related colleges like this one originally attracted students who lived only a buggy ride away. Students were dropped off in September, maybe after the harvest was well along and Dad and the horses could be spared for a day and the student for a few months. No college needed a parking lot in those days. A hitching rail was enough.

I'd explored the town the week before, when I'd first arrived, and had found much that was endearingly similar to other college towns I'd known. On both sides of Main Street, down the hill toward the center of town, were great old wooden frame houses, front porches wrapped around them, in various degrees of elegance or decrepitude. A mattress hung out an upstairs window of the Omega House, one of the local fraternities. A dog lay on the front porch. (Golden retrievers or black labs, heads on their paws, seeing all and telling nothing, have replaced the housemothers of yesteryear.) A lawn mower, chewing into a summer's worth of grass, had been abandoned in midmow.

At the foot of Main Street was the commercial center of town. If you turned left, drove past the post office and past the town's only bed-and-breakfast, you got to the interstate in a mile or so—it went south to the state capital, north to Chicago. If you didn't turn left, but parked your car and walked along Main, you'd pass the city hall, a beauty shop, a hardware store, a bank, a grocery, and the Edgewood Inn, which wasn't really an inn but a smoky bar that served pretty good food with familiar ingredients. No radicchio here.

Everyone gathered at the Edgewood Inn—the chief of police, members of the city council, the mayor, who also ran the liquor store, students and faculty from the college, farmers, and an occasional truck driver. My first college teaching job had been in a village like this one. Faculty and students mingled everywhere. Very cocurricular.

Middleton was too small and its citizens probably too poor to support a Wal-Mart or a discount mall. It still had the charming small-town aura of earlier times. It was the kind of place where children could safely leave their bicycles on the front lawn overnight.

This morning I crossed Main Street from my office, nodding to the administrative smokers on the building steps.

"It couldn't be a nicer day," I said.

"That's why we don't quit," said Fred Farnsworth, the dean of admissions, grinning almost guiltily. "We'd miss the fresh air."

The morning had a familiar rhythm. At 8:50 a.m. students emerged from residence halls and classroom buildings and the dining hall. They walked in small groups, dressed informally in shorts or jeans. T-shirts commemorating rock concerts and the Hard Rock Cafés of the world. An occasional nose ring. One kid had a tiny silver figure climbing up the rungs of his earrings. Nobody was making a personal statement with hair length or style, except for one senior woman who had shaved her head. I already knew about her. Her best friend was undergoing chemotherapy, and she'd shaved off all her hair in sympathy and solidarity. An admirable gesture of friendship, I thought.

You could tell the RAs (resident assistants—the housemothers' successors in residence halls) because they wore tie-dyed shirts for easy identification. Nice kids, eager to be helpful.

The new students were warily checking each other out as they headed to class, not subtly, but not moving toward obvious pairings yet either. They'd known each other only for a couple of days, since new-student orientation. Most looked sleepy. One big guy yelled a welcome to another across the quad: "Hey asshole, I thought you weren't coming back this year." I couldn't hear the reply.

At nine o'clock, the college bell pealed; the scurrying ended; students went into the buildings. Then it was quiet, except for the Weed Eater neatening up the graves in the college cemetery. At 9:50, doors opened, more scurrying. At ten, all quiet again.

The pace was familiar. It hadn't changed much since I'd been a college freshman—excited and fearful, alternately boisterous and withdrawn. My parents, proud that I'd gotten a scholarship, were worried that I was too young to leave home, but they let me go anyway.

I had never left college since my own opening day, except for undergraduate summers and the year I'd worked to save money for graduate school. I was a true believer. Small colleges like this one, and like the others where I'd spent most of my career, were a uniquely American invention, and I loved them. Many young people (like me) who'd have floundered in a big university were able to succeed at places like this—not the brand-name colleges, which did different things for different kinds of students, but the small, often church-related places on a hilltop, with faculty dedicated to teaching and to opening the life of the mind to young people who'd never even heard that phrase before.

Places like Middleton, at their best, wakened kids to the possibilities of their lives—how the world works, how we think the universe works, how they could live lives of meaning. Sentimental stuff these days. Still, the first day of class seemed like a time of undiminished possibility to me.

One thing was different about this opening day. Among the groups of students and faculty headed to class or breakfast or wherever were visitors from the outside world—from the real world?—from the media. Television cameramen, in sweat-soaked undershirts and grubby shorts, followed perfectly groomed reporters in well-cut suits (not a nose ring among the lot), roaming the campus. Occasionally they'd stop a group of students, extend a microphone, then move on.

They had one question: Did the black students return to Middleton College for the fall semester?

I had another question, just for me, never uttered aloud. Could I preserve order and safety this year, and could I keep the college from further public humiliation?

~

Nearly five months before, on an April evening, a racial incident had occurred at Middleton College that had brought national attention. A fight with racial overtones had taken place.

Two students, one black and one white, were injured badly enough to be taken to the local hospital to get patched up. One lost two front teeth; the other received a deep facial cut.

A crowd had gathered quickly that night, forty or fifty students, full of beer but not fall-down drunk. Baseball bats were brought out but not used. The crowd divided along racial lines. They called each other names. The police came and dispersed the crowd, and most people went home to bed.

In the days that followed, however, matters became worse, not better. Many of the black students left the campus, saying they didn't feel safe, and they wouldn't come back until their demands were met. The long-serving president retired under pressure from the board and the faculty, and several key administrators resigned.

To outsiders, it might have seemed that a tiny cause had produced mighty effects. To those who knew the college well, it was clear that the incident was only a flare-up of grievances that had been smoldering for a very long time.

Nearly a year before, the trustees had invited a higher-education consultant, Gerald Petosky, to campus to help them plan for the future of the college. His findings had included serious concerns about racism: racist attitudes among student leaders in the residence halls, for example, and racial hostility in town.

An all-college planning committee, building on Petosky's work, had identified a number of minority issues that deserved attention: Middleton needed more minority students, more minority faculty and staff (there were none), and more multicultural courses in the curriculum.

During a campus convocation, several months before the crisis, black students had expressed serious concern about the way minority students were treated on campus. No one had responded, then or later, to their discontent.

There were other warning signs, too: an interracial dating

relationship gone bad, in which a white woman went before the Judicial Board alleging assault by her black boyfriend; the punishment that was meted out, a suspension for the rest of the semester, was considered unduly harsh by many of his black friends.

Then, the night before the April Incident, a female student told her friends and her RA that she had been abducted and beaten by four men on a back corner of the campus, and the administration had done nothing to allay or acknowledge or investigate the allegations. She didn't indicate the race of her alleged attackers, but word quickly spread that they were black. A few days later, she admitted that she had made up the story.

In the early morning chill on April 2, fires were set in trash baskets at either end of a floor in Foxcroft Hall, which housed both men and women. The Middleton Volunteer Fire Department responded. Students waited out in the cold while the smelly, smoky fire was extinguished, and while they waited they talked about the alleged assault of the night before. That night, the April Incident occurred.

I didn't know any of that background in the spring, but long before I ever thought I'd be coming to Middleton, I'd read about the incident in the *Chronicle of Higher Education* and *The New York Times*—not the sort of papers that usually cover news from a small college campus. Both had pictures. The *Chronicle*, a weekly newspaper of record in higher education, showed a group of black students milling around outside a residence hall. The *Times* had shown a group of white fraternity brothers, seated on the front steps of their house, looking very Joe Cool. Very white.

Odd. A man-bites-dog story. Trouble in paradise. Students at a small church-related liberal-arts college in the middle of the Midwest started some kind of racial fight. From the information in the newspapers, the affair didn't make sense.

A week or two later, the *Chronicle* had another story: the black students had left the campus, saying that they didn't feel safe at Middleton College.

Now, in August, the media had returned to see whether or not they had come back, and what Middleton College was going to do about its racial problem. After they had collected student impressions and faculty opinion, most of them stopped by my office.

I welcomed them warmly. Tried to, anyway. With as much charm as I could muster, I explained to one and all that twenty-three black students had left the campus early last spring, not the fifty-four black students enrolled then, and eighteen had returned. To most of the reporters, this seemed a distinction without a difference. If a single student felt unsafe on this quiet campus, that was news, and it was deplorable. My version also made the story more complicated, because it implied that not all the minority students were of one mind about conditions at Middleton.

One of the national dailies sent out a photographer and a reporter for a follow-up. The photographer asked for separate pictures of two black students and me and told us where to stand. I posed, smiling and leaning against a campus oak. The two black students, one male, one female, posed, one on either side of a very white pillar. They did not smile, although the young man looked, somehow, as if he wished he felt more like smiling. The young woman was more grim, close to anger. She spoke for both of them: "It was hard to come back here," she told the reporter. "But we needed to make sure changes were brought about. We said, 'Well, if we're not here, who's going to make sure Middleton won't go back to the way it was?' "

I am, I said silently. I am. That's why I came.

Actually, when the invitation came to serve as interim president I hadn't hesitated. Was that foolish? I'd just completed a difficult presidency, and I wasn't sure I wanted another. I didn't have a clear sense of what had happened at Middleton, but I'd learned during my first visit to the campus that nobody did. Many versions of the April Incident circulated around the campus and village. Something small had gotten bigger; more and more cameras had come; and a group of worried parents had taken their children away from once-sleepy Middleton. Administrative heads had rolled.

I came because of the racial problem, because I was curious, because I was sure I could help, and because I cared a great deal. Like millions of Americans, I believed deeply in equality, and I had cheered the civil rights movement of the 1960s, but mostly from the sidelines. I had tried to find an effective way to put my convictions to use.

"Multiculturalism" and "diversity" were words that were never uttered in their present meanings when I went off to college in the early 1950s. "Diversity" meant a few black students, a few foreign students, but mostly kids from different parts of the United States—slightly different accents, sometimes close to dialects. Hearing those accents had made me feel cosmopolitan, as though I were entering a much more complex world than I'd ever known.

Well I was. The only diversity I'd known before I came to college was maybe having a family down the street where both parents worked outside the home, or where a widower was raising his son alone, or where a woman had been divorced and didn't die of the shame or move away.

In my childhood neighborhood, those sorts of diversity were talked about among the people my mother and father knew. When another kind of diversity got closer, we moved. We needed a larger house. We wanted to be nearer to Minnehaha Parkway. The postwar housing shortage was easing. Our family could afford it.

I had no black friends until I went to college. They were called Negroes then. I knew Martha best, probably because she was from my hometown, and we rode the train together at vacation time. She was a bright student with a great aptitude for science. She wanted to go to medical school, but her color, she believed, made it impossible or at least unlikely. (Though we didn't talk about it then, being a woman made it nearly impossible, too, in those days before the civil rights movement and affirmative action.)

Martha majored in speech therapy instead. Her advisor, well respected in the field and a terror to her students, told Martha things like "You people tend not to be hard workers" or "You people won't get ahead unless you get your term papers in on time," as though Martha were somehow bearing the burden of responsibility for racial progress in America.

The same professor revealed her insensitivity—or was it cruelty?—in other ways, too. In my freshman year, a student with cerebral palsy, leaning heavily on two Lucite canes to walk, came trembling to the front of the class to give her final speech of the semester and fainted dead away. Canes clattered; Paula crumpled. In a few seconds, when Paula showed signs of life, Professor Baffin nodded to two students to help her and then called on the next speaker.

Luann, another black classmate of mine, was elected May queen by a vote of the entire student body. The newspaper in this midwestern community always published a photograph of the May queen and her court (the two runners-up) on the front page. The editor decided it was inappropriate to picture a black queen and two white attendants. The president of the college negotiated a compromise: they would be photographed, but wearing classroom attire, not regal robes and crown.

During my first Christmas vacation home from college, I had a party for the college classmates I knew who lived in the Twin Cities. Neither Mother nor Dad objected to inviting Martha. Her father drove her over. They got lost on the way to my house and arrived late. Mr. Avery returned to pick up his daughter when the party was over.

These simplicities of arrival and departure brought out the anxieties my parents felt but had concealed from me. "I hope they didn't stop too many places in the neighborhood to ask directions," my mother said the next day. "I wish she hadn't pushed the curtains aside to watch for her father," she added. "That was rude."

In the fall of my sophomore year, my father came to my college for Dad's Day, and a group of us went out drinking. I'd rarely seen my father in a party mood before. He was an austere, hardworking patriarch who rarely smiled and almost never laughed. But that night at the Rathskellar we sang old drinking songs and told daring dirty jokes in front of our fathers. Because our dads were paying, we daughters ordered drinks we'd never had before—exotic drinks like Tom Collins and Singapore Slings—and passed them around the table for all to sample.

"I didn't like that," Dad told me later, now returned to the austere self I knew better. "That Negro girl drinking out of your glass." Somehow, in college, like so many young men and women of my generation, I came to have different ideas about race than my parents had. I even argued about racial injustice and inequality over Christmas dinner, until my father astonished me by pounding the well-laid table so that the sterling jumped and the water goblets tottered. "I suppose the next thing you'll want to marry some Negro," he shouted.

"Non sequitur!" I retorted, indignant at his illogic, confident that my rational discourse would carry the day, or at least the dinner hour.

Of course it didn't. He sank back in his chair and shook his head in an attitude of despair.

"We've always taught her to speak her mind," my mother said hopefully, at the same time patting my knee under the table. This meant, Don't speak your mind anymore just now. Someone changed the subject.

Later in my college career, at the next Christmas dinner, I

expressed an interest in taking some courses in the psychology and sociology of race, to understand racism better. That day, a more learned guest at the table capped the well: my aunt, who was a junior-high-school geography teacher and who'd been present at last Christmas's blowout, observed, "Don't you think those academic disciplines are far too new to give us a sure grasp of important issues?"

I forget my reply, but her remark did achieve its purpose—a preemptive pat on the knee, and successful in its intent. I never did take any such courses and settled instead into a major in international relations. I learned to talk about other subjects at the family dinner table—only slightly less disruptive: what a great president Adlai Stevenson would make, and what a menace to democracy the House Un-American Activities Committee was—but I never stopped paying attention to racial issues. When I decided to go to graduate school, I chose to study American history.

I earned my advanced degrees in one of the great graduate history departments, at the University of Wisconsin, and married a fellow graduate student. I chose the university because Merle Curti was there, and I had been told that he took women graduate students seriously.

This was, after all, the 1950s. Many professors at many elite institutions prided themselves on having never "taken" female graduate students. Somehow this added to their professional luster. At first that struck me as funny: arrogant old men, afraid of women with brains. Then it made me mad: arrogant old men with power over women's lives, afraid of women with brains.

In those days at the University of Wisconsin, there was no such thing as black history or black studies, or black professors, and only a couple of black students. One of the professors in the department, well respected for being a distinguished graduate trainer (we were all being trained, like thoroughbreds for the track, expected to bring honor to the university whose silks we carried), was admired for his ability to turn students who had attended humble undergraduate institutions into first-rate writers and researchers. His measures were harsh, we agreed, but effective. To one black graduate student he shouted, "When are you going to learn to write like a white man?" That professor didn't take women either.

In my first teaching position, at Colgate University, which was then a men's college, I don't remember any black students and certainly no black faculty. After all, Colgate had just recently hired its first Catholic, and I was only the second woman. The first was the president's wife. (She was always referred to as "Everett Case's wife" or "Owen D. Young's daughter," Mr. Young having been an eminent financier who helped revise the plan for post–World War I reparations. To refer to her thus, in those years before the women's movement, meant that she was doubly distinguished.) Both she and I had part-time contracts, and my husband, like hers, was a full-time employee of the university. It was nepotism for sure, but okay, we tacitly understood, as long as it didn't happen too often.

Some faculty members believed that black students or faculty shouldn't be permitted at all. A colleague in my department, a courtly man of southern birth who had lived and worked in the North for thirty years, once explained to me why it was so important to maintain Jim Crow in the South. His chivalrous nature made it difficult for him to be entirely direct, but as nearly as I could figure out, the need for segregation had something to do with toilets, venereal disease, and the likelihood of its spread from black women to white.

Nevertheless, the times were changing. The civil rights movement was gathering strength and support in high places. Desegregation was becoming the law of the land, and many of the old inequalities were being swept away. Or maybe only under the rug.

It was a proud time to be in higher education. The sit-ins, the voter registration drives, the freedom schools, were all conducted by college and university students, black and white, from North and South. Some of them paid with their lives for their commitments.

I was still pretty much a bystander. By now I had two young children to care for. I talked equality in my classroom, but I lived in upstate New York, and classroom discussions about racial equality were cheap and easy. I watched the March on Washington on television and wished that I were there.

Our family—the two children; my husband, Kent; and I—did go to Washington five years later, for professional reasons. Kent needed a summer of research in the National Archives, and I was finishing up a writing project that required some work at the Library of Congress. We chose to live on Capitol Hill, in a racially mixed neighborhood.

The year was 1968, the summer after the assassinations of Robert Kennedy and Martin Luther King Jr. Black citizens had rioted in Washington in the spring. In July, the Poor People's March, planned by Dr. King, went on as he had intended. Mule-drawn wagons from all over the region slowly converged on Washington and camped near the Lincoln Memorial. The leaders of the movement hoped this would bring the War on Poverty to the forefront of legislative attention.

We could feel the tension in the city as the encampment grew. Helicopters hovered noisily over our neighborhood two miles from the tent city, and squad cars by the dozens parked at the curbs along East Capitol Street. One night a busload of National Guardsmen sped past our house. Everyone feared more riots, but they never happened. Rain and mud and manure added to the misery and despair of the campers. The leaders were still quarreling over who deserved to inherit the mantle of Dr. King or whether, indeed, it was even a mantle worth having.

When the wagons went away, they left a quagmire behind that was quickly sodded over by the skillful (mostly black) groundskeepers of the National Mall. By the end of the summer all traces of the wagons and the mules had disappeared.

My children had black playmates for the first time in their young lives, and David, age seven, learned to swim at the neighborhood pool where he was the only white child in the class. His best friend, Larry, was black; his father was a janitor at the Capitol.

"If Larry had a bath," David said to me one evening as I was preparing dinner, "he'd be the same color as me, wouldn't he? Just like the palms of his hands."

Wow. I realized how isolated my children had been from people of color.

Capitol Hill in 1968 was full of people who were trying to create a genuinely integrated neighborhood. Many were young professionals or academics like ourselves. Many of us were living amid the threat, and often the reality, of crime and violence for the first time in our lives. Nearly every week the local Safeway, just around the corner from our house, was held up by an armed gunman who then made his escape down our alley.

At that, it was a more innocent time than today. Then, armed gunmen rarely fired if the victim obeyed their orders. Today, in the same city, one is likely to be shot anyway. Many white middle-class families living on the Hill in 1968 were also living for the first time among poor people and people without hope. We saw them sitting listlessly on their front stoops, night after night, in the oppressive heat and humidity of Washington. I was glad when the summer ended.

Late in August we went back to our home, now in Minnesota, where the minority population was about four percent, but where residential segregation kept that four percent thoroughly separated from the white majority. I joined a community group in St. Paul that had persuaded the school district to bus children from black and Hispanic neighborhoods to white schools to achieve integration. Our group provided the kinds of services we thought were necessary to make busing work. I drove mothers to parent-teacher conferences. I tutored fourth graders in reading and math.

Ironically, the neediest student I tutored, Walter Foster, was white. Walter's older brother had been killed two years before in Vietnam, and his grief had overwhelmed his ability to learn. His highly educated parents, one a university professor, the other a member of the school board, were distraught that Walter was doing so badly. They remembered his brother as a brilliant student. Each evening Walter's father sat down with his surviving son so that they might read the newspaper together and thus improve the boy's reading skills. Perhaps this comradeship helped them both.

I never knew. I never knew what happened to any of the students I tutored. Strangely, embarrassingly, as I think of it now, it never occurred to me to wonder how many of my other young pupils were learning impaired because they had lost siblings in a war that disproportionately affected black Americans. Many years later, at the Vietnam Veterans Memorial in Washington, I found the name of Walter's brother, etched in the black marble. He was the only person I knew, even faintly, who had died in Vietnam.

By the early 1970s, the growing national grief and rage about the Vietnam War were overwhelming much that was good in American life and stunting the movement toward racial equality. The nonviolent phase of the civil rights movement was over.

Still, much progress had been made. In the classes I taught at Macalester College there were now both black students and white. A course I taught on the Civil War and Reconstruction took on remarkable new life and interest when nearly half the students were black. The historiography of the period had greatly changed since I was in graduate school. New scholarship emphasized how reluctantly the Great Emancipator had decided upon emancipation, and how Reconstruction could be considered a golden age for black Americans.

Historians were beginning to talk about the contemporary civil rights movement as the Second Reconstruction. I found it exhilarating. History mattered. Students got angry about one interpretation or another. They had strong opinions about the idols of the past.

A few years later, when I went into college administration, not long after I was divorced, issues of race were high on the agendas of colleges and universities, and issues of gender equality began to contend for resources and public attention nearly everywhere. By now a body of legislation existed to protect minorities and women from discrimination, and administrators ignored it at their peril. Federal and state agencies stood by to enforce the laws, with varying degrees of vigor and lassitude, depending on the political climate of the day.

The promise of equality and justice was not the impossible dream it had been in the 1950s.

~

By noon of opening day I decided that things were going well enough. The dining hall was noisy. Most of the reporters were gone. They rarely stayed for scheduled events, I soon learned, except press conferences and athletic contests. Opening convocation lay ahead.

I'd given considerable thought to the convocation, my first official speech to the college community. It would set a tone, a standard, a goal for the year. Faculty and staff lined up for the academic procession outside the auditorium. We were splendid but moist in our caps and gowns.

Another procession had preceded ours—Coach Lombardino and the entire football team, assistant coaches at the rear like tough Border collies, occasionally growling, ready to head off a stray, getting the boys seated in the back rows where they slumped and sprawled. "Coach always makes the team come," Bonnie Truesdell, the dean of students, had told me in advance. "It shows his commitment to academics."

Football was very important here, and despite the fact that the college was in Division III of the NCAA—could award no athletic scholarships, for one thing—many young men came to Middleton to play ball. They certainly didn't come because the college was a conference power. Middleton had had a losing record for decades. Except the year before! The Middleton Wildcats had won the conference championship for the first time anyone could remember, and it had been an extraordinary moment for everyone connected with the college. The doormat of the league, the everlasting underdog, had triumphed at last.

The team was huge. If Ohio State had the same percentage of its students out for football it'd have a team of more than four thousand. I'd already encountered some of the gridders in the dining hall before college opened. They were rude and boisterous, elbowing up to the milk machine, regardless of who was in the way. Like me. They traveled in groups, from residence to dining hall, and they didn't respond to a cheerful "Good morning" from a passerby. Like me. Perhaps they were like old-time sailors, fearful that a woman on board would bring bad luck, and that speaking to one might sink the vessel.

When I'd met the retired president, Phil Harkness, a month or so earlier, I'd asked him what he thought could be done to restore racial peace. Still stung from all that had happened to him after his years of faithful service, he'd replied caustically, "Play football all year around."

After we'd processed into the hall, Bryant Dunbar, director of multicultural services—a new position and a new hire, in response to one of the demands made in the aftermath of the April Incident—gave the opening prayer. The vice president for church relations had retired, and the position was not being filled. I told Bryant I was giving him instant ministerial status, a battlefield commission, and we'd both smiled.

He sounded appropriately ministerial. Heads bowed at his command. He succinctly invoked God's blessing on our college. A raggedy "Amen" came from the audience. Heads raised. Maybe a third of the student body was there, between two and three hundred students, scattered around except for the bunch at the rear. Some looked bored already. A few were still in the attitude of prayer, snoozing. A few looked attentive. Maybe the attentive-looking were faking it. Maybe the bored-looking were trying to be cool. My speech was short. Fifteen minutes was as long as one could expect to hold an audience of students. Part of me wanted to call out to them, It won't be long. Just concentrate for a few minutes. It's really going to be interesting. I hate boring speeches myself, and I wouldn't dream of delivering one.

I didn't say any of that. I gave my speech, "Back to the Future." I invoked the mission of the founder of Middleton College, to build "a coeducational Christian college for students of all races," a radical mission in pre–Civil War America—so radical that the state legislature, then in the hands of proslavery Democrats, wouldn't approve the college charter. Now let's get back to those founding principles. Let's polish them up again, like we polished up the Founder's Plaque. Let's fulfill the promise that the founder saw for this college, and for America, and that was forgotten for a while.

Applause followed; not thundering, but adequate for my sense of well-being.

The audience stumbled through two verses of the old abolitionist hymn "Once to Every Man and Nation," now updated with inclusive language at my request, "Once to Every Soul and Nation." We recessed, and the pulse of the day continued, marked by the hourly peal of the college bell.

CHAPTER 2

August and September: Assessing the Damages

When Phil Harkness retired, he asked that he be permitted to remain in the official residence on campus for a few more months, and the trustees had agreed. They had rented a house for me in Jefferson Mills, a small town twelve miles away. As I drove home that evening, I reflected on the day. The college didn't seem about to explode, but there was an intangible air of tension on the campus, a walking-on-eggs quality I had felt coming from some students, especially white students.

Several important changes had been made during the summer. I hoped they'd be enough to get us through the year without trouble. I couldn't be sure. The Board of Trustees at its May meeting had authorized spending $100,000 to play multicultural catch-up. Two black faculty members and a director of multicultural services had been hired; the college had agreed to establish a Multicultural Center and a student-faculty diversity committee. Sensitivity-training sessions were to take place early in the fall semester, for faculty and staff, and for students in each living unit. To allay concerns about student safety, agents from Security Inc., a private firm, were hired to police the campus night and day.

I drove on, past the football field, where the team, with many black members, was still at practice. The bleachers and the running track around the field were in poor repair. The track was asphalt. You don't see many of those anymore. Frost heaves had broken up the surface in many places. Rather than spend money it didn't have to fix it, Middleton had dropped track and field as an intercollegiate sport several years before.

The campus and the town shrank behind me. The two-lane road led past cornfields and pig farms, all of them too small to support a family. Somebody had to have a job in town for sure. The farmhouses were small, worn and weather beaten like the bleachers.

Many of Middleton's students came from places like these. They and their families struggled to pay the college bills and relied on federal loans and college grants to get through. Lots of kids, I'd already discovered, defaulted on their student loans. Part of the problem came because freshmen were encouraged to take out loans before they had any idea whether or not they could (or wanted to) do college work. Then, after a semester or after the football season, many of them melted away, leaving their indebtedness and no forwarding address.

A college can lose its eligibility for federal student loans if the default rate becomes too high. Some historically black colleges and universities are exempted from those regulations, but Middleton College, with a minority population of eight percent, was not. Losing eligibility would be a disaster.

I shook such a worry out of my head as I neared the outskirts of Jefferson Mills. When I reached home, I drove the car into the garage and pronounced the opening day a success.

~

I already knew that Middleton College had worse problems than loan defaults, but I needed to know much more than I'd read even in the generous supply of materials the presidential search committee had sent me. That would help me decide what my agenda for the year ought to be—what I could hope to accomplish. The trustees expected me to present a set of priorities to them by the time of the homecoming meeting of the board.

They didn't want just a caretaker. They knew by now that Middleton had serious problems in academic and student life, and they wanted me to start fixing them. Many members of the board weren't certain that personnel changes had gone far enough.

My cabinet, the vice president and deans, could do only so much to help me understand the needs of the college. I'd talked to the finance vice president and the dean of admissions back in July, so I had some sense of financial realities, but to learn about faculty and students, I'd have to meet with them directly.

Maybe I could also correct misinformation and rumor, still around from last April. Even though media coverage had been abundant, no two stories were alike. In the absence of a consistent account of events, rumor had attained the stature of fact, and reporters, when challenged about their use of unsubstantiated rumor, would shrug and reply, "Perception is reality."

Reporters and photographers had roamed through the residence halls night and day and had entered classrooms willy-nilly. No administrator dared say they couldn't, lest even worse things be written about the college.

I needed to keep anything like that from happening again. I would try to open communications with every group and build up a level of trust, on campus and off. That's what presidents are supposed to do. It might be harder here. I knew absolutely no one before I came, except (slightly) the members of the search committee that hired me. I was also the first woman to head this college, and thus doubly an outsider and a focus of attention.

I wanted to know what everybody talked about (besides me): what their fears were, their hopes, their expectations.

No mass meetings, though. I wouldn't have any of those.

I'd seen videotapes of two that had been held in the spring, and they weren't pretty. Student leaders (white) sitting in the front rows on one side. Kids yelling, temperatures rising, nobody in charge, an RA turning toward the black students, who were all sitting together on the other side of the auditorium, pointing her finger at them, and prefacing every angry sentence with "You people."

I had already met with the first group, the faculty and staff, the week before classes began. About sixty people came to that meeting, including a few emeritus professors who still lived in town. The demographics of Middleton's faculty were unusual. Turnover was extraordinarily high, and it had been like that for years. The national average was about four to five percent annually. Middleton's was either twenty-two percent or eighteen percent, depending on whose numbers you believed.

Many new instructors were hired each fall, some of them still graduate students at the state university. There was also a sizable number of very senior faculty who had been at Middleton for many years. There was almost no midlevel faculty. To put it another way, if Middleton were a family, as President Harkness used to affirm, it had a missing generation—no parents, only grandparents and children. When you finished your graduate degree, you left. Grandmas and grandpas stayed behind, some content and happy, some living disappointed lives, haunted by their long-dead aspirations.

The meeting had been in the Founder's Room, the most elegant on the campus, where the Board of Trustees met and where potential donors were wooed and refreshed. Above Victorian love seats were the portraits of past presidents and, of course, the founder, Phineas Lowell. Floor-length mauve velvet drapes hung at the windows. Two large, dark china closets held antique cups and saucers, sterling-silver candy dishes, and souvenir spoons (the commemorative T-shirts of their day) from cities far away.

Rows of folding chairs had been set up, very close together, for this meeting.

What do I need to know about Middleton, I asked in effect, and what do you want to know from me?

The grievances ran from great to small, but none were about race. The older faculty were in their late fifties or early sixties. They'd been spectators or participants in the civil rights movement, I guessed. The younger faculty, the new ones, had grown up in a desegregated, affirmative-action world. Nobody here thought it was dangerous for whites to sit on toilet seats where blacks had sat or sip from the drinks of black friends.

What did they think about race, though, here and now? What did they think should happen here? That was more difficult to figure out. When troubles had come in the spring, and when the black students left, faculty had been extremely helpful in making arrangements for them to take their finals at home or in deferring finals or canceling finals and giving grades on the basis of work already done.

When, after the first couple of days, the crisis had continued to grow, the faculty had convened in the auditorium while students marched outside—carrying signs, shouting for administrative change—and had voted no confidence in the president.

When they did that, they were pretty sure he was on his way out, or they might not have taken the risk. Though an affable man until the troubles came, Phil Harkness had held the college tightly in his control. Middleton had no tenure system as commonly understood in higher education, and the college had been on the censure list of the American Association of University Professors (AAUP) for ten years, as being in violation of rules of good practice in higher education. The absence of the protection of tenure, and rumors of the swift departure of people who disagreed with the president, kept dissent to a soft growl.

Now he was gone or at least out of office—I wondered who

visited him now, or phoned him. Maybe the deans? The vice presidents? He surely had friends, after fifteen years at Middleton, and some of them must be in this room. There was something a little unsettling to me about the fact that he was in residence on this campus and I was not. Silly. I was the president, and he was not. He also had enemies in this room. Grievances had accumulated over the years: merit pay inconsistently awarded, promotions denied, heavy teaching loads unrewarded, contracts dithered with to the disadvantage of individual faculty members, retirement promises unkept.

In addition to personal grievances, the faculty had concerns about students. Student quality had gone way down, some of the old-timers observed, and student consumption of alcohol had gone way up, especially in the sororities and fraternities. Drinking started Thursday and kept on through the weekend. I knew that wasn't unusual. That happened everywhere I'd been, even on campuses where liquor was forbidden.

I did hear something new:

"Can you do anything about the bannings?" asked Jane Proctor, a senior member of the English department.

"The what?" It wasn't easy to keep the note of incredulity out of my voice.

"The bannings. People get fired and they can't come on campus anymore. They're banned."

"What happens if they do?"

"Well we don't know, except one person who lives on campus and works for the college invited a banned person to dinner, and she was fired. Except she got her job back a couple of days later, and the president said we made too much fuss about banning."

"How many people are in a banned status?" I asked.

"Lots."

"We don't know."

"Three or four."

"No no, many more than that."

A kind of eagerness swept the room—indefinable, as though they were opening the door to the Heart of Darkness, or lifting the bandage from the worst wound, or acknowledging the worst indignity. All of the above.

"What have these people done that gets them . . . banned?" I asked. I could hardly say the word. What an unfortunate choice of terms. It smacked of Afrikaner rule, but here it apparently had nothing to do with race. Could it have racial consequences? None of the black student activists had picked up on it. It seemed like a natural term to beat the administration with, but apparently that hadn't happened.

"We don't know," said Professor Proctor.

"I'll look into it," I concluded.

And that was pretty much how the faculty conversation went: people eager to tell their stories, hoping for better days, but not regarding racial issues as central to their discontents. I did look into the bannings. I searched the files and found only three confirmed cases, not one of whom seemed like a public enemy. I sent letters to each and a memo to the college community: The statute of limitations has run out on banning, this is a new administration, so come to campus whenever you like. Actually I was more cautious, you might even say mealy-mouthed: "You will not be unwelcome," I wrote.

Members of the administrative and support staff—men and women such as financial aid officers and admissions recruiters, accounts payable clerks and alumni relations personnel—were a little more guarded in their questions and comments than the faculty. On most campuses such employees are indispensable: they answer the phones, they bring in new students, they raise money, and they make certain that everybody gets the right check on payday. On most campuses, they make the college operate effectively (or not), and they are usually held in low esteem (or worse), especially by the faculty. On many campuses, administrative positions have multiplied in the past twenty years, while faculty numbers have remained pretty much the same. That's a source of friction. Was that true at Middleton? The friction? It didn't seem to be.

Another surprise: Most staff members had no job descriptions because the college had been encouraged to think of itself as a family—family members don't have job descriptions; they do what needs to be done. So ran the rationale. Some staff members were uneasy about that. How could their performance be evaluated? Answer: It couldn't. It wasn't. At least not in any face-to-face way.

Fortunately I didn't have to argue that issue with anyone, because the ADA (Americans with Disabilities Act) had already made that rationale unacceptable and obsolete. The starting point to bring an institution into compliance with ADA is to provide job descriptions for every position. We were just starting to put those together. We'd ask every employee and supervisor to define the positions in their departments.

Low salaries were a great source of frustration among administrative staff members. Few job opportunities existed in town or in the surrounding villages. The college had a captive workforce. What could I do about that? Probably not much.

Again, nothing about race.

The student groups were tougher to meet with. I felt something different coming from them—fear, maybe; mistrust; not knowing what to say. Especially the men.

I went to Cutter first, the men's residence hall. The residents were mostly athletes, many of them wrestlers and football players. Middleton College was a wrestling power. The wrestling coach, Ed Jason, who was also the athletic director, had been at Middleton for many years, and his teams and the alumni loved him.

The so-called living room in Cutter Hall was about as livable as an armory. It had no newspapers, no magazines, almost no furniture. A large television set of ancient ancestry had been pushed into one corner. A few straight-back chairs, a couple of ersatz leather armchairs, were lined up in a row, facing a small lectern. That's where I'd stand to begin a discussion. Young men—mostly white, a couple of blacks—wandered in. They had big voices and punched each other amiably and whispered as they came forward. One would whisper to another. The other would give a raucous laugh.

(When I was sixteen years old and walked to high school past a bunch of young men lined up on the sidewalk, the performance was just the same. I never knew how to respond. There was no good way. If I kept walking, eyes front, I felt prissy. If I looked at them—they'd go *"Ooooooh"*—I felt wanton. In either case, raucous laughs were my reward. I always felt embarrassed. Now I was old enough to smile and shake hands. They were embarrassed.)

"Are you going to get us more money for football?" a spokesman asked. "That's why guys come here. The administration's building a fancy library with the money we should be getting. What can you do about it?"

Not much. Did it show that I favored libraries over football fields?

After a half hour of conversation, the room emptied. The young men shuffled away, most of them looking sour.

The atmosphere at the fraternities was more polite, the members more articulate, the environment even more spartan. One house couldn't afford furnace heat, so each resident's room had a kerosene heater. A common decorative touch in every fraternity was the flat wooden paddle. You've seen it: six inches or so wide, except at the gripping end, which is round for easy swinging, about thirty inches long. Lacquered, the Greek letters of the fraternity on one side, crossed paddles were often mounted over the fireplace or several might be hung on a row of hooks along the entrance hall.

The living room at the Alpha House, the first one I visited, was cavernous and open to the ridgepole. A fire several years before (nobody hurt) had gutted the interior and touched off an endless fund-raising campaign among Alpha alums. They still had a long way to go. The task of restoration looked impossible—on the magnitude of standing up all those trees blown over on the slopes of Mount St. Helens.

The Alpha brothers wore coats and ties for my visit, and they sat in a large circle. One black member attended. Middleton's fraternities and sororities were local, and they had always admitted students of color, a source of pride.

"Is it true that you're going to get rid of football? We heard that you were."

"No, I have no intention of getting rid of any sport. Who told you otherwise?"

"We heard you were. We heard you were going to give the athletics money to women's sports."

"I'm not."

Two weeks before my visit to the Alpha House, I had learned that a Title IX complaint had been filed against the college, alleging inequalities between men's and women's athletics, and harassment of women players and coaches. I had read a copy of the complaint, submitted jointly by several women coaches now departed and by a current male member of the physical education department. The complaint was no secret on campus, though few students understood what it meant.

I guessed that not one student in the Alpha House knew that there was a law compelling equality between men and women in athletics. What they'd heard, I suspected, was that somebody was going to take money from their sports and give it to women's sports. Since Middleton now had a woman president, she was the likely somebody.

I tried to explain, as I had asked the dean of students and others to do when I learned of the complaint, but with modest success. I wondered if somebody else was trying to keep the waters muddied. Paranoid thinking. Not appropriate, but the common cold of presidential leadership these days.

The other sessions with student groups were similar. Politeness at the sororities and fraternities, questions about athletics. Women coaches had not stayed longer than a semester or a year because the atmosphere was so hostile. This kind of turnover didn't build winning teams.

I love sports. I played high school basketball long ago, in the days when the rules allowed women to play only half the court and to bounce the ball only twice when dribbling. (An increase from one bounce in the junior-high rules.) I took up long-distance running when I was in my forties and now try to run three or four miles each day. I love what Title IX, imperfect as it is, is doing for women in sports. My daughter played varsity soccer in high school, and she set a record in cross-country at her college. I had a hard time concealing my enthusiasm and approval for the young women who spoke up in these sessions about the handicaps they faced at Middleton.

What about race? I began to hear cautious murmurs of indignation from the white students. They weren't mad at Middleton College or its black students, they said, but at the media. "When we tell people we go to Middleton, they say, 'Oh that racist place' or 'That place that had the race riot' or 'We heard about that racist place on television.' It's hard to straighten them out." Later, much later, I wished I'd asked them, "Do you think this is a racist place?" And I wished I'd asked the black students if they were mad at the media, too, or embarrassed at attending a racist place.

"Everything was blown out of proportion." I was to hear that sentence a hundred times over the next few months, but never from a black person.

I began to hear complaints about the sensitivity-training sessions, too. "They're shoving it down our throats," one young fraternity man declared. What was who shoving? Betty Dunbar, Bryant's wife, was doing presentations on racism and the black experience in the various living units. The goal was to sensitize white people to the ways they unwittingly showed disrespect to black people.

Sensitivity training had been around for more than twenty years. In the public-school district I knew best, back in Minnesota, it had come with school desegregation. All public-school teachers had to take some workshops or in-service courses in sensitivity training, so that they could more effectively teach the minority students who were now in their classrooms. Did it work?

I had my doubts. I remembered a teacher and a student from those days. One Sunday afternoon I took a black girl, Ladorra Miller, who loved horses as ardently as my young daughter did, riding at a nearby stable.

On Monday morning, Ladorra excitedly reported her excursion to her teacher, just outside the classroom door. "What do you say to Mrs. Kreuter?" Miss Halvorson at once replied, ignoring Ladorra's enthusiasm.

Silence.

"What do you say when somebody does something very nice for you, that she wouldn't even have to do at all," said Miss Halvorson, her voice growing more stern with each pointed hint. She had had the full sensitivity-training treatment, but it failed her now. She would never have thought to teach manners so testily to a white pupil from one of the "good" families in the neighborhood. In one exchange, she had lost Ladorra's trust and had muzzled her enthusiasm.

She effectively muzzled mine, too. If this was what lay at the end of the horseback ride, I didn't want to do it again, and I didn't. The whole thing had taken on a Lady Bountiful quality that repelled me.

But maybe sensitivity training was better than nothing, and

maybe it was more sophisticated now than it had been in those long-ago days. What could have been done instead? Right now I didn't know. So I just listened.

The final Q-and-A session took place in Foxcroft Hall, about two weeks after classes had begun. The atmosphere was different now. Was it that this time there were both men and women at the meeting? Significantly more black students? I couldn't tell. Amiability had ebbed, and a roughness of spirit had replaced it. The atmosphere reminded me of the videotape I had seen of the meeting held a few days after the April Incident. This meeting in Foxcroft wasn't out of control, and it wasn't about race, but students seemed angry at each other and at the college.

Complaints about athletic facilities were endless: the weight room, damaged by water and by generations of students dropping barbells, was in danger of collapsing to the floor below; the handball courts had been used as batting cages. I'd seen them: their walls looked like they'd been shelled by mortars.

Complaints about residence halls were abundant: deferred maintenance, leaky roofs, bad plumbing.

"See for yourself," one student suggested, and after the meeting was over I did. Murmurs and slammed doors rolled before my escort and me, like surf toward the shore, as I conducted a cursory inspection. The students hadn't exaggerated.

I was glad when the sessions were completed. They weren't fun. Especially as I sensed discontent, for all kinds of reasons, was just below the surface. That's what I had wanted to find out.

Now I could start making my things-to-do list.

~

No, not quite yet. A new top priority suddenly presented itself, a new embarrassment.

Ed Jason rushed into my office only a few days after the Title IX complaint became public.

"We have to give up the championship," Ed blurted, alternately shaking his head in disbelief and running one hand through his gray hair, "the football championship from last year." He was a thin, wiry man, about sixty, with a narrow face, usually sunny, now grim, forehead furrowed. He wore a Middleton T-shirt, a whistle around his neck, khaki pants, tennis shoes. I invited him to sit down and share some coffee with me. He shook his head even more insistently.

He poured out his terrible news. "We played an ineligible player. We have to give up the championship. It was an accident. We weren't trying to cheat. We just didn't have the records right on one of the guys. He wasn't really one of the stars or anything, but according to the league rules, they have to convert every game he played in from a win to a loss."

Ed and I had already had a conversation about the Title IX complaint. I had been the spokesperson to the media on that one, because it was easy for me to express my firm support of Title IX. Ed was glad to be free of that burden, but he was earnest in denying that sexism played any role in the athletic department. As for himself, he told me, "I'm as upset at being called sexist as I'd be if . . . if I were called a queer."

I let that remarkable statement pass without comment.

"We didn't need this," I said. A revelation of the obvious. "We'll need to send out a memo to everybody," I continued. "We don't want to have our people read about this in the newspapers. I'll let you look at a draft before I send it, but it needs to come from the president's office."

Once again, Ed looked relieved. He had done his duty. But that afternoon he came back to my office. "We found another one," he said earnestly. "Another ineligibility: it's a woman. She was a soccer player last year. We didn't do it on purpose. We just didn't keep the records right. We're doing it right now. It won't happen anymore."

I was pretty upset. Ed seemed to feel that uncovering another ineligibility proved that Middleton hadn't broken the rules on purpose just to win the football championship. The women's soccer team had lost every game!

Could Ed be permitted to stay on as athletic director? I couldn't prejudge the Title IX issue—I couldn't assume the college was guilty of sex discrimination. But how could I permit an AD to stay in office when he had been responsible for so egregious an error as the loss of a major championship? But how could I dismiss so beloved a figure as Ed? Nobody blamed Ed for what had happened; they blamed the league officials. "What should I do, Matt?" I called Matthew Austin in the state capital. Matt was the public relations consultant who had been hired to help Middleton last April when the PR director resigned. She hadn't been replaced yet—a search was under way—so Matt was still on a retainer for the college.

"Can you reassign him to other duties in the department," Matt suggested, "and appoint somebody else in the interim?"

"Probably, but what if he doesn't want to be reassigned and screams to the media about his many years of faithful service and how shabbily he's being treated."

"Try out the idea on him."

I did. Ed was thrilled. We called a press conference the next day, and after an hour or so of coaching from Matt (at Ed's request, so he wouldn't sound stupid, he said), Ed announced that he had decided to resign as athletic director. He was getting on in years, he said, and he had been AD for a long time. He would continue as wrestling coach—his first love—and he'd teach a couple of courses in the physical education department.

~

The reporters were kind. The next day there were warm appreciative remarks about Ed in the local papers and on local television. I heaved a sigh of relief. So, no doubt, did Ed, now honorably out of the limelight. In the afterglow of Ed's resignation, little media attention was paid to the fact that I had named a woman, Geri Schmidt, as interim athletic director. She was the obvious choice, the only person in the department who had any administrative experience.

A couple of days before, while my memo about the championship was being distributed around campus, I had walked down to the football practice field to talk to the team and the coaches. They already had the news, but I wanted to express my regret and my understanding of how disappointed they must be. Coach Lombardino whistled the team off the field, and while I gave my small speech of consolation ("You'll always be champions to us"), he shifted the wad of gum in his mouth and blew large pink bubbles at me. Coach was not going to be a friend.

For everyone on the team, losing the championship was a terrible blow. Some of the players had had to borrow money to buy the championship rings they wore, and they weren't about to take them off. Some members of the team had graduated or left school—they weren't even around—and many current members were freshmen who might have chosen Middleton College because it had just won a football championship.

Only the league record book would show what had happened. Who cared? Coach cared, that's who. He felt that his college should have protected him and his team better, not given in to the league. I cared for several reasons. It's terrible to have something taken away from you that you've worked so hard to achieve. It's terrible to become a media doormat and feel publicly humiliated by one thing after another. From my perspective, worst of all is that this might have truly been an example of sloppy record keeping, not deliberate deception. Where was there more? Now I had something else to look for.

~

The maple trees were beginning to turn color, and I welcomed the drive home each evening. Two miles south of Middleton I passed a small lake with an old-fashioned resort at the south end—individual "housekeeping cabins," and a rowboat with each. The cabins needed painting, and the plumbing probably didn't work very well. When I was a little girl growing up in Minnesota this was the kind of place we went for a week or two every summer. Aunts, uncles, and cousins came. The grown-ups went fishing (the men by day, the women by night, after the chores were done and the children were in bed); the children went swimming, or fishing off the dock, or, when we were a little older, rowing around in the boat by ourselves, looking for turtles or fishing for sunnies.

One day, when I was still too young to take the rowboat out by myself (something I longed to do) and when everybody had gone to town but Grandma and me, I caught the biggest bass of the week—or was it maybe even of the whole summer?—while fishing off the end of the dock. Grandma had taken a picture of me holding the fish. I still had the photograph in an old family album.

CHAPTER 3

September: Damage Control

On the first Sunday of the semester, I had gone to church in Middleton. Knowing something about the church to which this college was related was part of understanding the institution. It would help me set that agenda I was developing. The denominational church was on the campus, but it served the entire village. It was a large, sturdy structure, faced with the same stone as the college library and constructed at the same time. Intellect and spirit, side by side. The interior of the church was as cavernous as the Alpha House.

The pews formed a large semicircle around the chancel, and a stained-glass light fixture hung on a long chain over the altar. The bulb was burned out. A small, dim light glowed from the lectern, making it possible for Reverend Oswald to read his sermon and follow the order of service.

Only about twenty people were present that day. I recognized some of them—emeritus faculty and their wives and two or three current faculty members. The rest must have been townspeople: they knew me; I didn't know them. No students attended, and none of the younger faculty.

The service was dispiriting. No choir; a couple of familiar hymns sung at a funereal tempo; a couple of Bible verses read haltingly by Professor Emeritus Wenderley, who was legally blind. Reverend Oswald delivered a sermon that had no discernible relationship to either the hymns or the verses. I think it was about the power of prayer. The congregation was spread so thinly throughout the church that during the offering worshipers had to stretch to hand the collection plate to the next nearest person. I stayed around for coffee afterward and shook a few hands. Everyone was kind and friendly. I chatted with Dick Oswald, a small, nervous-looking man who listened expectantly to each parishioner who spoke to him.

"Do students ever come?" I asked.

He shook his head sadly.

"No, except for a few that sing in a choir we get together for memorial services or a few other special occasions—Christmas, Easter, baccalaureate. Most of the students at Middleton aren't of this denomination. The largest number are Catholic. I don't know if they go to Mass."

College students, no matter what their faith, aren't much for Sunday services.

"Was there ever a college chaplain?" I asked.

"Yes, but he left a couple of years ago."

"And wasn't there a vice president for church relations?"

"Yes, but he was supposed to be a fund-raiser—you know, he went around to denominational churches in the area and asked them to contribute to Middleton. He also sent them material on admissions. I don't know how successful he was. When he retired last year, they didn't replace him. I don't know why. I think the college brought in a black minister for a while last spring, to serve as a temporary director of multicultural services. I'm not sure what he did. I'm just the minister of this church, you know. I don't know much about what happens at the college, except what I hear from my parishioners."

One thing was clear: so far, at least, the church relationship had not played much of a role, for or against, in the college's troubles, at least not from the Middleton end. Rachel Harkness, the president's wife, had been an earnest supporter and volunteer at the church. Early in Phil's presidency, she had started the Nearly New Shop downtown, with one or two of the older members of the congregation, and it still did a brisk business.

Although this, the local church, seemed to have turned its back on the college—maybe out of necessity, or maybe it was a mutual turning of backs—the denomination, with headquarters in the state capital, was deeply interested in how it might play a role in solving Middleton's racial troubles. On my calendar early next month was an appointment with the human rights director, Marcella Winthrop. She was coming to spend a day on campus to assess the racial climate and also, since the Title IX complaint had been made public, to check out the gender climate as well. Then she might make some recommendations to me and to the Board of Trustees, and presumably to other denominational colleges, and to headquarters. I was looking forward to her visit. I was already starting to feel isolated, and hungry for contact with the world beyond Middleton.

Middleton College was not unusual in having had its cords of religious affiliation fray. Very few Americans felt anything like the fervor that had fueled the founding of these colleges a century and more before. Who, in late-twentieth-century America, would ride through dense woods for three days on horseback, as Reverend Phineas Lowell did in 1844, looking for the proper hilltop on which to plant his church and his college? Who would follow him? Probably not even members of his own family. (One can imagine the children: "Oh Dad! You've gotta be kidding." His wife: "Not when I'm just about to make partner.") What should the church relationship mean today, especially concerning racial and ethnic issues? I hoped Marcella could help me with that one.

I didn't have time to give much thought to the problem, and inspiration did not seem to lie readily at hand. When I left the church after the coffee hour and walked down the street to my car, the campus was still deserted.

The following week was unusually busy. In addition to the usual avalanche of meetings, speaking engagements, and curiosity appointments that come to a new president, there was another whole set of activities commanded by Middleton's special notoriety. On Monday I gave an interview to the Black Entertainment Network just before I gave the luncheon talk at the Middleton Rotary Club, and that afternoon I met with the regional director of the state Commission on Human Rights shortly before the interview with the editor of the college newspaper and the "Meet the Prez" meeting with nontraditional students and commuters.

All the meetings were exhilarating, and all the people I met were welcoming. The tension on campus that I had begun to feel during my visits to residence halls and Greek houses was growing more palpable, especially after the humiliating loss of the football championship. I had met with my cabinet the day before, on general college business, and no one mentioned anything out of the ordinary: money was short, and the freshman class was smaller than we'd hoped, the pace had quickened on finishing the new library, and all classes were adequately staffed. The Phonathon would begin next month. All requested materials in the Title IX matter had been sent to the Chicago office of the Department of Education. Campus thefts and break-ins—student rooms burglarized, musical instruments stolen from the music building, no one ever prosecuted—had decreased significantly since the Security Inc. service had been hired.

Near mid-September, shortly after I returned from a luncheon speech at the Women's Professional Network in nearby Echo River ("Shattering the Glass Ceiling") the assistant dean of students, Ginny Jones, came to my office. Ginny had graduated from Middleton only a few years before. She'd grown up on a farm nearby, and she had a ruddy round face and sturdy figure that I associated with country air and rural life. She majored in psychology and pledged Zeta Pi. I wasn't sure what she did in the student services area, but I did know she kept in close touch with her old sorority.

"I'm kind of worried," she said. "Maybe for no reason. I don't mean to waste your time, but I'm worried," she repeated. "The Zetas are going to expel their two black members," she said. "They've gotten a lawyer to write official letters to Holly and Ellie May. The letters are going to say that Holly and Ellie May violated the principles of sisterhood by going on the *Sally Jessy Raphael* show last summer and talking against their sorority."

I took a deep breath.

One of the most curious bits of fallout from the April Incident had been an invitation to four students—two black, two white—to appear on the *Sally Jessy Raphael* show, one of the bare-your-soul, trash-thy-neighbor television programs. Hard to resist an all-expense-paid trip to New York and a national television appearance, and they didn't resist! Sally's staff kept the blacks and whites separate from the moment they arrived. Holly and Ellie May had been given elegant lodging at the Radisson; the two whites, Esther and Phyllis, were billeted together in a no-frills room at the Days Inn.

Barbara Tuttle, Professor Tuttle from the psychology department, had told me that part. She had accompanied the students, entirely unofficially and at her own expense. She had been disgusted. "It was so clear those kids were being manipulated, encouraged to be hateful to one another, to make a better show."

I'd seen the videotape of the show. They weren't hateful, just numb with stage fright. Their voices were pinched; they barely moved their lips. Two minutes of Holly Washington telling her version of the April Incident in a monotone ("The guys came down the hall yelling 'Nigger' and the girls from Zeta Pi cheered them on"). Two minutes of Esther Parker, also in a monotone, eyes fixed on the camera, telling her version ("The black guys ran down the hall yelling threats to the white guys and they turned the corner by where the drinking fountain is") and then the announcer breathlessly breaking for a commercial: "In a minute, we'll return for more about race riots at Middleton College." To lead into and out of the commercial breaks, the sound track played crowd noises and popping sounds, like gunfire.

"How long has this expulsion been in the works?" I asked.

"A couple of weeks. Ever since Holly and Ellie May resigned from the Zetas."

"They've already resigned? What's the point of the letters of expulsion?" (It seemed silly. You can't quit; you're fired. Was that the idea?) "I'd like to talk to the president of the chapter," I said. "After the teddy-bear parade."

The on-campus child-care center had an annual Teddy Bears' Picnic, in which all the toddlers and their teachers marched from the center to the picnic grounds a block away, led by a celebrity grand marshal.

Today was the day, and I was the marshal. Everybody, adult and child alike, carried their favorite teddy. I confessed to the organizers that I had no teddy, favorite or otherwise, so Mrs. Brill, the head teacher, loaned me an ancient, threadbare extra. It had one glass-button eye and a few threads hanging where the other eye once had been.

Linda Weeks, president of Zeta Pi, was waiting for me in my office when the parade ended and I had turned in my teddy. She did not look friendly. She looked like my children did when they knew they were going to be scolded in a way they considered highly unjust.

"I'd prefer it if you didn't send those letters," I began.

"We have a right."

"Yes. You do, but I think it's going to cause no end of trouble."

"We have a right," she repeated. "They've dishonored the Zetas."

"Why did you get a lawyer? Don't you think that's provocative?"

"We wanted to expel Holly and Ellie May in just the right way, with the right words and all. We weren't trying to be provocative."

"I don't think that sending the letters is going to bring any credit to the Zetas," I suggested.

"The chapter has voted. We're going to hand-deliver the letters tonight." She pushed her chair back and stood up. Oh damn.

"I'd like you to take another vote."

She wavered. "I don't know, I'll see. We're having a meeting of the chapter tonight. To let everyone see the letters before we take them to Holly and Ellie May. I don't know."

Hurrah. A tiny victory.

As soon as Linda had left my office I made several calls. First, to Matt Austin: "I think you better come to campus this evening. We're going to need your help." Next I called Bryant Dunbar.

"Have you heard about this flap with the Zetas?"

"Yeah, from the Black Caucus. They've heard that Holly and Ellie May are going to get these letters, from some lawyer, throwing them out of Zeta Pi, and they've already resigned. They're pretty pissed. I don't know what they'll do."

After that I called Art Dove, Middleton's finance vice president who was also chief of security. "We might need some more Security Incs. on duty tonight," I suggested. Then I called Harlan Elliot, the academic dean and chief executive officer in the president's absence. "Harlan, we've got a problem that might erupt while I'm away tomorrow and Friday. I need to brief you about it."

Personally, I was troubled. I was going to be away for the

next four days, and not on college business. I was taking my annual long weekend with four old friends on the North Shore of Lake Superior. The occasion was so important to me that my absence for those days was written into my contract. Could I leave this campus in crisis? There were no telephones at Castle Haven Cabins. This seemed like it could be a serious matter, but I wasn't sure.

When Matt arrived, around 5:00 p.m., we decided to call a few people together to talk through our alternatives and await the outcome of the Zeta Pi chapter meeting. I asked Harlan and Art to come over to my office, as well as three members of the student services staff—Bonnie Truesdell, Bryant Dunbar, and Ginny Jones, who'd be our liaison with the Zetas.

We ate rubbery pizza Matt had picked up on his way into town and drank cans of Pepsi from the presidential refrigerator in the back room. We talked about likely outcomes and alternatives. We discussed what the college's official position should be, and what the media might make of the whole issue.

"We're being too passive," said Art. "We should take a position for the college right now. The president should go over to the Zeta House and tell the members that the action they're contemplating is racist, and they shouldn't do it. Nobody's ever been thrown out of one of the societies. Certainly not after they've left already."

"Has anybody seen the text of the letter they propose to send?" asked Matt.

"I have," said Ginny. "It's like how Holly and Ellie May disgraced the chapter by going on that television program to talk about what happened in the April Incident."

I was preparing to buckle on my presidential armor when the phone rang. Linda Weeks. Several of the Zetas had changed their votes. The letters would not be delivered that night. The crisis was not over, I knew, but the delay in taking action should defuse the situation. (Or was I just trying to make myself feel better for leaving the embattled college the next morning?) Our meeting adjourned about 9:00 p.m. I went home, packed, and went to bed.

Flying to Duluth on Thursday morning, I replayed the events of the night before. Some things were clearer than they'd been then. Bryant Dunbar had been left out of the loop in student services. Bonnie and Ginny had known this flap was brewing for two weeks, and they'd never consulted Bryant, never even told him. What had he known and when? Did he talk to Holly and Ellie May before they quit the Zetas, and if so, did he tell other members of the student services staff whatever the two had said to him? Should he have? More questions I couldn't answer. I dozed until the long flight finally ended. Peg, Jane, Annette, and Deb picked me up at the airport, squeezed me and the luggage in Peg's car, and set off for Castle Haven Cabins, fifty miles up the lake.

~

The view from cabin number 4, hugging the ancient rocks above Lake Superior, was as stunning as ever. From where my friends and I sat after dinner that night (no rubber pizza here), looking through the big picture window, we could see a spectacular electrical storm over the lake. Bolts of lightning flew from the sky to the ground on the South Shore, as though they were being flung, and layers of clouds sailed in opposite directions, up and down the lake at the same time.

"So why is this such a big deal?" asked Jane, after I'd recounted the previous day's events.

Looking at the weather outside, hearing distant rumbles and the plunks of large raindrops on the roof, I wondered a little myself.

"Sororities are stupid," said Peg. "Especially on a small campus. They just divide people unnecessarily. Why would anybody want to belong to one anyway? These kids sound pretty immature."

"I agree," I said. "But I'm not a nineteen-year-old college

student. I wouldn't go on the *Sally Jessy Raphael* show either, but these kids did, and maybe I would have when I was nineteen and it was my first trip to New York, and somebody else was paying for it. Especially if I thought I was striking a blow for racial justice."

"What do you think this flap is really about?" said Deb. Good question. I listened to a few more rumbles, watched another lightning bolt.

"I think it's really leftover racial tension that's hanging over the college, that nobody knows how to deal with. The tension is still there, even though the Old Regime is gone and the board appropriated some money to meet minority concerns."

"Are you surprised?" Peg asked.

"A little." Had I thought, perhaps, that the April Incident had been "blown out of all proportion," as other white people told me? Did some part of me think that the April Incident was just playacting? A childish squabble?

More likely, I'd had too exalted a view of my peacemaking powers. I really had thought that showing goodwill on my part would produce it in others.

On Friday the five of us hiked from Silver Bay to Bean Lake, a small jewel hidden in the woods, with a granite cliff jutting up from its north shore and a grove of yellow aspens shimmering at the east end. When we got back to Silver Bay, I called Harlan at the college. He told me what had been happening.

The letters had been delivered that morning to Holly and Ellie May, and the whole campus had known within half an hour. The Black Caucus had demanded that the cabinet meet and denounce the actions taken as racist. Harlan had stalled, probably wisely, and asked to see the relevant letters and documents. He scheduled a meeting for Monday—I'd be back by then—and promised a statement by late afternoon. The Black Caucus was willing to wait.

Hallelujah.

That night was clear on the North Shore. We built a wood fire on the rocks and sat close to it, enjoying its warmth, telling our stories to one another. Up and down the shore, we could see other small bonfires. On the lake, an occasional ore or grain boat passed, lights gleaming festively in the night, headed down the lake to Duluth, or eastward to the world.

Shortly before dawn, after a good night's sleep, I sat alone on the front porch of cabin number 4; I could see the constellation of Orion bright and clear in the southern sky, and the moon in its last quarter. The universe seemed to be in good shape, behaving predictably.

Surely I could take care of my tiny corner of it.

~

At 3:00 p.m. on Monday, I convened the cabinet and started the meeting. "What shall we do about this?" I asked.

"I feel the same way I did last week," Art began. "We've got to make a strong statement." Art was about thirty years old, the youngest member of the cabinet, mistrusted by some board members because of his youth. His dark, pinstriped suit somehow made him look younger still. Every so often he'd scowl, turn his head, and take hold of the collar of his starched white shirt, as though it didn't quite fit.

Art had worked for an accounting firm after he graduated from Middleton, then returned to the college as controller three years before. When the chief financial officer left, or was fired, or took sick leave, nobody was sure which, Art took her place. He was doing a good job, and he wasn't afraid to speak out, as he had last Wednesday and again now.

"Quite a few alums are members of Zeta Pi," said Alice May Peterson, director of development, "and some of them are pretty good givers. I don't think they'd like their sorority getting a reprimand over this. After the Sally Jessy thing, I received several letters from alums."

"About what?"

"Well, about the poor grammar that the students used. The alums were wondering about the quality of the college now." Those were fair concerns, I thought, but they were also ways of commenting on race without saying so.

"No matter what we do, it's not going to improve student recruiting, especially if we make the television news again," said Fred Farnsworth. Although Fred was dean of admissions, he'd been a little bit of everything in the last few months, ranging at will over the whole campus. When I had come for my interview in June, I thought Fred had been named acting president. No, he'd just acted like one. He had friendships with several of the board members, and they welcomed the news he brought them about conditions on the campus. They trusted him to tell them the truth, and they were probably right.

He was no General Haig leaping to command. He was trying to make things better for Middleton College—that was good—and he was bored with his own office, admissions; that was bad. The months of crisis in the spring were critical months for recruitment of new students for the fall, a time to rally the recruiters and exhort them to bring in the class, but that wasn't what Fred liked to do, and nobody told him he had to.

Bonnie and Harlan said little during that meeting. Each time someone else spoke, they looked to Fred to see his reaction. They were the cabinet members who had been closest to President Harkness, and Harkness had warned them that their jobs might be in jeopardy when he left the college. That was true, but for more complicated reasons than he had implied.

By 3:30, when four members of the Black Caucus arrived to press for a decision from us, we had decided. The cabinet and the president deplored the action of the Zeta Pi sorority in expelling its two black members.

I read aloud the memo we had hastily drafted. The Caucus members listened quietly, thanked us respectfully, and left.

I next met with the leadership of the Zetas and read them the same statement. They listened glowering, their faces in expressions of increasing disgust. They left muttering to one another.

I would have no friends at Zeta Pi.

More troubling was the fact that the college had no control over the doings of the Zetas or any other of the sororities or fraternities, and neither did anybody else. Yet they were located on the Middleton College campus, and all their members were Middleton students or alums. The college could hardly avoid being associated with whatever they did.

This time, however, at least in terms of media response, Middleton was home free. Nobody, black or white, had called them, and 3:30 was past television deadlines for filing stories in time for the evening news. By tomorrow this would be old news, cold and stale. The story was also about a sorority, about conflict only between women, and it had nothing to do with sex or athletics. A yawner.

Monty Pettigrew, the president of the Panhellenic Council, was waiting in my outer office. Monty was so clean-cut he seemed made from poster board. He smiled indulgently. "You and I need to talk," he said. "I want to help you, so you don't get off on the wrong foot with the Greeks."

Which foot would you like me to apply to the Greeks, I thought, and exactly where?

"Thank you!" I said. "Another time, perhaps. My secretary can make an appointment for us."

I closed the office door, returning Monty's indulgent smile as I showed him out, and started going through the neat little stack of pink telephone messages that had accumulated while I'd been gone. At 6:00 p.m., I took a couple of frozen burritos from the fridge in the back room and zapped them in my microwave. The bust of Elihu Tompkins Sloane, chairman of the board, 1927–1945, looked on from the top of a file cabinet. He had fallen off his shelf when the library wall had collapsed, and he'd been in the president's back room ever since. Someone had put a yellow hard hat on him, and I'd left it in place. He'd be going back to the library as soon as his niche was completed. For now he was my dinner companion.

Before dark, I locked up my office and started for the parking lot. "Could I see you for a minute?" Patricia Epson, an admissions counselor, caught up with me.

"I'm really worried," she said. "Has anybody told you about what happened to Sally Murphy? Her folks live in town. Her dad is going to the police if somebody doesn't do something. He says he doesn't know what's become of Middleton College, and he's ready to call the police."

"What happened?"

"Two weeks ago his daughter Sally—she's a freshman and I recruited her. I think that's why her father has talked to me. Two weeks ago Sally was in her remedial English class—she's the only girl—and one of the guys unzipped his pants and took out his penis and wiggled it at her. She was really upset. She was so embarrassed she didn't want to tell her parents. She only told her mother, but her mother told her father the next day.

"Where was the instructor?"

"She was writing on the blackboard."

"How large is the class?"

"Six people I think. Sally's the only white person in the class."

Oh damn. Another black man/white woman incident, potentially the most inflammatory kind of confrontation.

"When do you think Mr. Murphy intends to go to the police?" I asked. He didn't have to go to the police, of course. "Can this wait until tomorrow, or should I try to call him tonight?"

"Don't call him tonight," said Patty. "He'll be working. Wait till tomorrow."

"Thanks," I said.

I called the dean of students after I got home. "Did you know about the Sally Murphy incident?" I asked Bonnie.

"Yes. Harlan sent her to me. Sally had told the instructor, right after class, and she suggested that the academic dean should be told and suggested she write out her account of what had happened. After he read it he decided it was a student services matter. I had a full calendar that day when she came to me, but we got together the next day."

"Do you believe her? Do you think it really happened?"

"Yes. She was very convincing. I told her what her options were. She could go to the guy and tell him she didn't like what he was doing. Or she could wait and see if it happened again and then tell him. Or she could bring a sexual harassment charge against him, and we'd convene a special judicial hearing. That would mean that many more people at the college would hear about the incident. She said she'd think it over."

I was certain that by now everyone on campus must know some version of the incident.

"Have you heard from her since then?" I asked.

"No, I don't think so."

"And you haven't called her."

"No, this is her issue. She has to decide."

"I gather from Patty Epson that she hasn't decided yet, but her father's pretty angry about the whole thing."

"She has to decide."

"I wish you had told me when you first learned about the allegation," I said.

I called Hugh Murphy the next day and told him I'd just heard about this matter, and I'd like to talk with him about it if he had the time. Both he and his daughter came that afternoon. He wasn't angry, at least not then, but he seemed mystified.

"I was so glad my daughter could go to college," he said, "and right here in town. I don't have a lot of money, but Sally got financial aid, and she can live at home. They've been so nice to her at Middleton, helping her in this remedial class so she can be a better writer and all. Then this happened. I never heard of something like this. And nobody's doing anything about it. That kid should be thrown out. He should be in jail."

Sally seemed strengthened rather than embarrassed or intimidated by this discussion. "I'm going to bring sexual harassment charges against him," she said.

Her father looked morose. "To think that my daughter should have to go through something like this. . . ." His voice faded.

"It's okay, Daddy. This is college."

Hugh wouldn't go to the police; I was sure of that.

In the end, a judicial hearing was held. The accused did not deny that he had unzipped his jeans, but he alleged—and the classmates he summoned as witnesses affirmed—that he had not taken his penis out. He was put on probation for the rest of the semester.

Bryant Dunbar told me that the young man seemed baffled by the proceedings. He had just been kidding around in a boring class. What's the big deal?

~

Tyrone Cartwright stopped by the financial aid office, where he had worked part-time, to say good-bye to Edna Holmes, the associate director. He was leaving college. His grades had made him ineligible for the football team, and he had family responsibilities to look after.

I had first heard about Tyrone from Bryant Dunbar. A few days ago, the police had stopped and searched his car at 2:00 a.m. in the center of town. The reason alleged for stopping him was that one of his taillights was out. The officer had found marijuana in the glove box, and he put the student in jail. Tyrone was black. Bryant came to bail him out and was kept waiting for hours, on a bench at the station—until the police had "verified his credentials." "You can have the prisoner now, *Dr.* Dunbar," Officer Beasley had said sarcastically as dawn brightened the sky.

Now Tyrone was leaving Middleton College. An hour after his departure, Mrs. Holmes screamed and called the police. Ten thousand dollars' worth of student loan checks were missing from the top of her desk.

CHAPTER 4

October: Helpers

The police assumed that Tyrone had taken the checks. They were sure of it when another Middleton student reported seeing him and a friend in the local bank, each cashing a large check, within a few minutes after he had left the college campus. The teller had been hesitant. When the student called "Hi Tyrone," the teller saw that the check he had endorsed was not made out to a Tyrone.

But Tyrone was off and away before he could be apprehended and questioned.

Chief of Police Janowicz shook his head wearily when he met with me later that day. I could hear him coming before he got to my office. He had a slow, heavy step, and he clanked and jingled like Wyatt Earp. No spurs, but the handcuffs and revolver at his belt created sounds I associated with the OK Corral at showdown time.

"I told your financial aid people last year," he began, "that they had to be more careful about leaving money lying around. They're just asking for trouble."

"You're right," I said. "What chance is there that he'll be apprehended?"

"Hard to say. I've put out a bulletin to the state police—wanted for questioning. You better tell Edna to stop payment on the rest of those checks."

"Are the news media going to find out about this one?"

"Sure. The theft's been reported; it's on the police blotter. That's where they go first for news."

"Is there any mention of Tyrone there?"

"Nope. Just that there's been a theft."

Chief (he preferred to be addressed by his title) went on to the financial aid office to talk to Edna Holmes, and I waited for the telephone to ring.

I didn't have long to wait. The outside world was ready to elbow its way onto the campus again.

The media, as everyone in America knows, are easy to dislike. They thrive on conflict, try to produce it when it doesn't exist, and make it larger than life when it does. They had no stake in Middleton College, except as a source of news, though they would have cried crocodile tears if their relentless coverage brought the college to its knees.

Phil Harkness believed they had brought him to his knees—had cost him his job after fifteen years of devoted service, just when the crowning glory of his career, the new library, was about to be finished and dedicated and maybe even named after him.

On the other hand, could the media have played so decisive a role if there hadn't been troubles here to begin with? Certainly not. The troubles, however, were complicated, and the media tried to make everything simple. Readers and viewers wanted simplicity. The "sound bite" was a symbol of simplicity. I had quickly learned to predict what fifteen-second phrase of mine would be chosen to be telecast from a fifteen-minute interview, and it wasn't far from that to crafting sound bites for myself in advance. Who wouldn't? But then I was tacitly giving in to the wish for simplicity. Why not? Because then I wasn't being true to the reality of the situation.

I was beginning to have this argument with myself on a daily basis. Sometimes I tried to imagine an ideal interview with a sensitive and informed reporter:

"Could you tell our viewers," I imagined being asked, "just

why you think Middleton College has been in such turmoil over the last several months and why there have been so many newsworthy crises? Take all the time you like to explain, and speak slowly. Our viewers are willing to listen to you for at least thirty minutes, and they like to take notes while they listen, so that they can reflect later on what they've heard. Sometimes they meet with their neighbors to have roundtable discussions of the key points our interviewees have raised."

I would begin: "First of all I think we have to understand the nature of small liberal-arts colleges and how their roles and their leadership and their needs have changed in recent years."

No, that's not the way. Try again: "First of all, we need to look at the demographics of our students and our faculty, where they come from and what their expectations are."

No, that's not a good start. "In order to understand the present crises at Middleton College, we need to look at the ways in which race, class, and gender are intertwined here."

No, that would take much longer than thirty minutes.

At this point I usually drifted off to sleep, or my imaginings were interrupted by hunger, thirst, or the telephone. My attention span, I thought ruefully, was much shorter than thirty minutes.

~

The media were not the only outsiders who were interested in what was happening at Middleton College. Agencies of the federal and state governments, nonprofit organizations, legislative caucuses, service clubs, church groups, and civic groups all wanted to know more. I had to assume that their intentions were honorable.

Early in October, Bryant Dunbar and I drove over to the capital to discuss Middleton's racial climate at the request of the state Commission on Human Rights. On the hour-long drive we talked about the college. I was concerned that Bryant was being isolated from the other administrators who reported to the dean of students. The faculty wasn't being very welcoming either. At a faculty meeting, Bryant had presented the plan for sensitivity training and for measuring the racial climate, and his remarks had not been warmly received.

The problem was not solely because of Bryant's race. In general, faculty members are not at their best in groups. Most college professors learn their group style—the faculty-meeting and committee-meeting style—in graduate school. In one's graduate seminar, presided over by a professor who largely determines one's professional future, the unspoken but universally understood purpose is to seem brilliant yourself and to humiliate your peers. There are a hundred degrees of humiliation, from the most obvious and inescapable to the wittily subtle. Once out of school, faculty members often conduct these exercises for their own pleasure, or maybe just out of habit.

Administrators are common targets. Most professors believe that administrators are useless impediments to teaching and learning, the source of many memos and little of value. Bryant roused their latent hostility: faculty members do not like having anybody from a (their opinion) lower-status unit (student services) tell them what they must do, especially someone like Bryant, who had an Ed.D. degree (a lower-status degree), not a Ph.D.

"Are they giving you a hard time?" I asked. Does water run downhill?

"I can handle it," he said. "They don't bother me. I'll do my job." He smiled. He was a handsome man just under forty years old. He'd played football as an undergraduate and still had the trim, firm body of an athlete. He'd been on the multicultural services staff of a large private university thirty miles from Middleton, and because his wife still had a job there, and his five children were all in schools that they didn't want to leave, he hadn't moved to Middleton.

So far that was working all right. Many faculty, and some

staff, didn't live in Middleton. They drove in from Echo River or Jefferson Mills, or from as far away as Chicago.

Their absence did change the nature of campus life. After 9:00 p.m., when the evening classes were over, very few adults from the college were around, except the Security Incs. and a couple of professors who liked to drink with the students and keep up with the news.

Bryant and I made our presentations before the Commission on Human Rights and then were invited to a catered lunch in a quiet dining room. The food was excellent, the atmosphere jovial. Our presentations had gone well. I had listed the actions taken by the Board of Trustees before my arrival, and Bryant had described the present environment for black students at Middleton.

"Would you say that the climate for minority students is improving at Middleton College?" asked Chairman Harrison, an old warhorse of the civil rights movement and of legendary crotchetiness. "I'm asking Dr. Dunbar," he added, glaring at me, to nip any inclination I might have to respond.

"Yes sir, Mr. Chairman," said Bryant. "I believe our students of color are much happier with their situation than even a month ago. Middleton is a better place for them."

"And why do you think that is?"

"Because we're doing the right things, and we have strong support from the highest administrative levels."

The whole experience was uplifting to me, and the drive back to Middleton was even better.

"You're serious about this stuff, aren't you?" Bryant asked as the cornstalks and pigpens flashed by.

"What stuff?"

"The minority stuff. You're not just trying to make things look better. I've never worked for anyone before who was really serious about it. No white person."

That was a good day.

The day that Marcella Winthrop came from the home office of the denomination had been a pretty good day. She had met with Bryant and the members of the Black Caucus first, and they had reported that things were getting better. They felt safe, they felt more comfortable on campus, and for the first time since they had arrived as students, they had some black role models.

Marcella talked to many students. Or she tried to. White students weren't much interested in discussing race relations.

"This diversity stuff is being shoved down our throats," one exasperated young man told her. "I'm sick of it. I don't want to talk about it anymore. I just want to go to class and play ball and spend time with my girlfriend. What's wrong with that?"

Before she left town, Marcella had a clipboard full of notes. She asked me about the status of women on campus, and about the climate for gays and lesbians, and about people with disabilities.

(A story lingered in the lore of the denomination, and Marcella retold it on that afternoon, about the paraplegic minister who had come to campus for a conference a year or two ago and could find no handicap-accessible bathrooms at Middleton College. He had had to drive fifty miles home to relieve his distress. I had heard the story before, and I confess that my mind focused less on Middleton's failure than on the fact that he had been able to contain himself for so long.)

"We've got handicap-accessible bathrooms now," I reported, "and curb cuts on all the campus streets, and handicap parking spaces. We've got a task force studying what else we need to do and how much it will cost. We have a long way to go before we're in full compliance with ADA. It's expensive."

"It's the law," Marcella observed, "and it's the right thing to do."

"No argument there," I said. But her words rankled. A few

days before, a student with a varying disability—one that required her to walk with crutches some of the time, and without them at others—had called the president's office: the "President Only" parking space was one car width nearer to the sidewalk than the nearest "Handicapped Only" space was. She had called the television station in Echo River, and it was sending a crew to videotape her and the parking lot. Presumably they would interview me about my indifference to the disabled.

"Tell Charlie to change the signs around," I had told my secretary, "and then call channel four and tell them there's nothing to take pictures of."

That memory was fresh, but I didn't tell Marcella about it. Not all the disabled are as winning as Tiny Tim.

"I think it's hard to be even a straight woman on this campus, much less lesbian or gay," I said. My mind returned to the discussion at hand.

"Why is that?" Marcella asked.

"Because of the gender balance here. It's pretty unusual. The percentages are about thirty-five percent female and sixty-five percent male. Most small colleges have more women than men—maybe fifty-five to forty-five. Not here. And so many of the young men are athletes or fraternity members or both. There's an *Animal House* quality to the campus. Men competing for women, women regarded as sex objects and accused of being lesbians if they don't like that kind of attention. It's very much like the 1950s. Worse, actually. In the fifties, being sexually active wasn't the norm as it is now. Then it was easier for a woman to say no."

I continued: "Some of the faculty, especially the women, try hard to help their women students resist the atmosphere. Not easy." My private thoughts: Was *I* doing enough? Was the dean of students doing enough? What kind of problems was Sally Murphy having with her classmates, after she had decided to press charges of sexual harassment? Did the problems fall along racial lines? Whom could Sally talk to? Shouldn't someone have organized a support group or a committee to promote a campus-wide discussion of sexual harassment?

"Professor Henderson, Jill Henderson in the sociology department—did you meet her?" I asked. Marcella nodded vigorously. "Jill does many things with her women students. She meets informally with a group of them to raise their consciousness about women's issues. She took some of them to Chicago last weekend to work on Carol Moseley Braun's campaign for the Senate."

Jill and I had talked about forming a commission on the status of women at Middleton College, but neither of us had done more than talk about it. Neither the dean of students nor the academic dean seemed interested, and I was reluctant to make them take it on. Should I insist? I wondered.

"And Professor Proctor in English has her students read Virginia Woolf, *A Room of One's Own*, and *Three Guineas*, at least. I don't think Woolf's very easy for them," I concluded.

"Do black women participate in activities or classes like that?" Marcella asked.

"I don't know."

"What's your guess?"

"Probably not. But I truly don't know. That's the stereotype after all—black women stand by their man; feminism's for white people. I haven't seen much evidence of sisterhood across the color line here." Or anywhere. I thought of the Zetas, and of Sally Jessy Raphael trying to sharpen the conflict between black and white women.

"Gays, lesbians, and bisexuals? What kind of a place is Middleton College for them?" Marcella was still taking notes.

"Not good, but not entirely taboo," I replied. We had a lecture on safe sexual practices as part of freshman orientation. One faculty member—she acknowledged to me that she's a lesbian—told me about the difficulties gays and lesbians have here. "They don't 'come out' exactly, although one of the fraternities has both men and women members, and everybody on campus seems to understand that most of them are gay."

Marcella smiled genially and put the clipboard in her canvas carryall. "What an interesting opportunity you have here," she concluded. "What are you hoping to accomplish before you leave?"

Nothing like saving the whopper question for last.

"Ask me next week," I said. "I'm presenting my official agenda to the board then. They should hear it first. It's taken longer than I'd hoped to put something reasonable together."

"I think you're doing a wonderful job here," Marcella concluded. "It can't be easy.

"It's challenging," I admitted.

"I'll be back in the spring," she said. We shook hands.

I was disappointed by our discussion. For some reason I'd never asked her *my* questions. What *should* the role of the church be here? We hadn't talked about that at all. What were other colleges of the denomination doing about race and gender issues? What were they doing about sexual preference? Were they just heaving huge sighs of relief that Middleton's problems weren't theirs?

Answering questions from outside examiners like Marcella was a new experience for me as a college president. I'd been through accreditation reviews for colleges, and I'd been on teams that conducted them. Supposedly these accreditation reviews were deep and probing looks at the institution being examined, but in fact they were usually quite gentle. "Peer review," as it's called, means that when I'm reviewing you, I will probably remember that my own college will be up for review in a few years, and even though you probably won't be reviewing it, some of your friends will. I probably won't be as critical as I might. I'll probably give a few quiet suggestions to the president and say nice things about the president to the board members I meet.

I knew of one college trembling on the brink of bankruptcy that had been given a clean bill of health. No, not a clean bill, only kindly instructions to return to the examining physician sooner than usual, to have its vital signs rechecked.

I'd been on accreditation teams that received anonymous phone calls and entreating messages slipped under hotel room doors, urging us to look at this or that. Sometimes we did, but we never thought the offenses were as grievous as the entreaties suggested, and we seldom mentioned them in our reports. I'd been on one accreditation visit to a struggling, failing small college, where the academic vice president had recently died of a heart attack and the president looked like he might have one at any minute. Our team was welcomed by the president as wise physicians and understanding friends, and indeed we were.

I'd been critical of peer review. One hand washes the other. Not conducive to maintaining high standards, I thought. Not probing enough.

The conversation with Marcella made me think again.

I'd rather be questioned, I decided, by a team of interim presidents, preferably women, from small colleges that had had racial troubles. I'd like to get together with them about once a week, in some location where none of us would be recognized. I'd tell them everything—about Tyrone and Sally Murphy and the football team—and they'd nod with warm understanding. They'd make an occasional suggestion drawn from their own experience. Such peer review didn't sound so bad. It might even be in the best interest of the institution.

Unfortunately, there weren't any peers like that around.

The next group of outside helpers that came to Middleton College were the Title IX examiners, one woman, one man. I expected to like them, and I did. Before they began their day of on-campus interviews, they paid a courtesy call to the president.

A few months before, I'd been a major speaker at the annual meeting of the American Academy of Sports Medicine in Dallas. I spoke on the history of women in sports, games, and athletics, and as partial compensation for my address, I'd been given a handsome framed certificate. I had hung it in my office, well before the Title IX examiners arrived. It was quite large, and the print was very clear.

"I can't help noticing . . ." the first examiner began, nodding toward the certificate, after the pleasantries of introduction were over. Just as I hoped. Surely my speech, before such a group and on such a topic, would establish my credibility as a supporter of all that Title IX stood for.

Of course it did, but that wasn't the issue. The question was whether or not Middleton College discriminated against women in its athletic programs. Still, the fact that this president liked sports and thought that women ought to participate in them should help a little. They interviewed students and faculty and coaches all day, one at a time, in a small room in Cutter Hall that had only a table, two chairs, and a very small window. A place where you might be questioned, I thought, en route to a gulag.

Although their report would not be made for several months, I heard, via the ever-lush grapevine, that they were surprised at what they had found by the end of the day. They were accustomed to investigating complaints on campuses that had substantial athletic facilities, kept in good repair, mostly for the men. At Middleton College, the facilities were poor for everyone. That's why the men were angry when they had learned there was something called Title IX, and they'd have to share their meager resources with the women.

Did the men, coaches and students, I wondered privately, believe that if they made things unpleasant enough for women athletes, they'd go away and at least leave the crumbling athletic resources to the men?

The Title IX complaint had been initiated by a woman

coach, and her account of her treatment at Middleton was devastating. Her troubles had begun, she claimed, even before her first day of work. Rumors were spread on campus that she was a lesbian. The evidence? She had not worn high heels to her job interview. Isolated, insulted, treated to small offenses that grew larger as time passed and her teams lost, she had finally resigned—as several other women coaches before her had done. Then she had written the complaint.

Could this have been avoided? Almost certainly. According to her complaint, she had repeatedly brought her concerns to several people in the school's administration. They had made vague promises to "look into it," but nothing had happened.

Now Middleton College, with slender staff and stretched budgets, had to respond to as many questions as a major university—the University of Nevada/Las Vegas, for example, or Ohio State—would have had to do if charged with such violations.

"We probably won't have a final report to the college until spring," the chief investigator told me at the end of the day. "We'll look forward to seeing you then."

On Saturday, I went to the football game. Middleton was playing Lakewood College on a slaty gray day, cold and windy, with a few early snowflakes in the air. Fans were wrapped in plaid blankets or huddled in thick down jackets, hoods pulled far forward.

Until this fall, for many years I hadn't been to football games where you felt the wind and heard the huff and grunt of players on the field, and saw divots of sod thrown up by the cleats of passing runners. No giant-sized players, no domed stadium, no artificial turf here, no huge television screen on which you could see the action much more clearly than by looking at the field. This was the charm and excitement of small-college football. You saw the reality of the game.

Football is a strange reality, though, and an unusual kind of game. A religious rite and a test of courage. The team ran onto the field, by twos and threes, holding hands. Then they dropped hands, fell to one knee, removed their helmets, and bowed their heads in prayer.

Prayer was definitely in order. Each player knew that members of the other team would try to injure him badly enough that he couldn't continue. The better the player, the more danger he was in. As the first half ended, the body count was two to one; Middleton was ahead: a broken leg and a concussion. The leg went to the hospital; the concussion was inhaling oxygen and begging to go back in the game. His mother, who was sitting behind me, was exhorting Coach to put him back in the game.

How much did it cost to put a uniform on one of these players?

How much did it cost to provide health-care coverage? What could the women's sports program do with even half the resources allocated to football? What could I do to strengthen the women's athletic program without heightening campus tensions? I could be a fan, of course, an equal-opportunity fan.

~

The justice department of the federal government was also trying to help Middleton College—actually it had been trying to help since April—and Bruno Altman, regional director of the community relations division of the justice department, called me near the end of October.

"Didn't want you to forget I'm here in case you need me," he said.

I'd met Bruno back in August, at a special meeting of the Middleton Board of Trustees. He had first been brought on campus last spring to assist in negotiating an agreement between the black students and the administration. At first President Harkness had declined to accept help from a bargaining group made up of Bruno and his colleagues. As the days had passed, and the crisis didn't go away, Harkness had acquiesced in the group's offer of assistance and conflict resolution. The director of affirmative action at the state university had also joined the bargaining group. After many days of discussion, an agreement was reached. But with whom? A president who had resigned, and several black students, none of whom would be enrolled in the fall semester, and none of whom had been elected or designated by anyone, except themselves.

Nevertheless, the black students who had left the campus before the semester ended in the spring had said they would not return unless the administration met their demands and reached an agreement. The agreement had been reached back in July, but without consulting the college attorney, Jack Sweeney, who was also a board member. When he was asked to review the document, the day after it was completed, he refused to approve it. He said it included policy issues that only the full board could endorse. Board members could look at the agreement in October, at their next regular meeting.

I hadn't met Jack then; I was still at my cabin in Wisconsin, in touch only by telephone with the college of which I'd just accepted the presidency. I recognized the strategy that was at work here, though. A common one in organizations. The administrator negotiates with an interest group, yields important ground, then says, Oh, sorry, the board (or the boss, or legal counsel) won't let me do it.

Curtis Havel, chair of the Board of Trustees, had called to tell me Jack's opinion. I found it worrisome. Certainly all parties thought they were negotiating in good faith and that they had been tacitly empowered to do so. Did the presence of a justice department negotiator lend an official status to the proceedings? No board worth its salt would agree to that, and I wouldn't even suggest it.

October was a long time to wait, though. The board's inaction might well be seen as a breach of faith and another example of the same old delaying and denying tactics that had gone on for years. That wouldn't be an auspicious beginning for my presidency.

"Could we call a special meeting of the board, to take place before college opens?" I suggested to Curtis. "We could have a thorough discussion of the points of the agreement, but we could still make an announcement about it, maybe even before registration. That would surely show the board's good faith."

Curtis was a thoughtful man, soon to retire from an executive position with a regional real estate firm. Recently remarried, he had cared lovingly for his first wife, who had been an invalid for many years, and when she died she was buried in the college cemetery. Curtis had reserved a plot there for himself. Phil Harkness had first awakened Curtis's interest in Middleton College, and Curtis had been generous in helping to establish the real estate concentration in the business department.

Last year's college Christmas card, which always featured Phil and Rachel Harkness surrounded by an annually shifting group of friends and family, had included Curtis and his new wife, just to the right of Phil and Rachel.

When the troubles erupted on campus in April and it became increasingly clear that Harkness would have to go, Curtis Havel called on him at home and told him he must resign. "Doing that was very difficult," Curtis had said as he told me the story when we first met. "It was my duty. He wasn't doing a good job anymore."

Curtis agreed to call a special board meeting, in August, shortly after I'd accepted the presidency, and most of the trustees were able to attend. Some of them hadn't met the new president yet, and that lent a special interest to the proceedings. We invited Bruno Altman to come as well, and we also invited Phil Harkness. He, after all, had represented the administration in crafting the agreement.

He was quite willing to come, and even more willing to meet with me in advance to discuss the meeting.

Phil and I devised a strategy to get the agreement passed. This is what we'd do: He'd characterize the importance of the document, the concerns of the African American students (the term they preferred), and how those concerns had been met in this document. Then I'd indicate my support of the document and applaud it as a statesmanlike piece of work. Factions in the board would come together as they saw the harmony between old president and new. It would be a love feast. The agreement would pass in a swirl of good feelings. It didn't work out that way.

How naive. Just for starters, Phil Harkness was silent and expressionless, while debate, not good feelings, swirled around him.

Jack Sweeney, with a toothpick at one side of his mouth while he talked, explained what was wrong with the agreement and why the board should vote it down. I shuddered.

An hour of discussion followed. Everyone present wanted to express their views of race relations, of separatism versus integration, and of the outgoing president. Everyone, that is, except Dr. Lillehammer, the oldest member of the board and a distinguished brain surgeon, now retired. He had brought his class picture with him—Middleton College, class of 1931—a panorama photo. He rolled and unrolled it several times, finding his youthful self anew with each unrolling.

Though I sat quietly for a long time, wearing the Mona Lisa smile I had cultivated in a previous presidency, I was getting panicky. The agreement was going to be defeated.

"Ask me my view," I entreated Curtis in a whisper.

"After everyone has their say," he whispered back. Mona Lisa's smile was hardening. On went the conversation, with no shaping direction from the chair. Finally I interrupted.

"I need you to empower me to carry out the operational parts of this agreement. The students are waiting. Perhaps we can defer the policy issues until the next meeting." I had just thought of that.

Dr. Lillehammer raised his hand first and was recognized by the chair.

"I would like to read a trenchant editorial from the *Christian Science Monitor*," he began. "It is about the importance of higher education to our future as a democracy." The reading of the article, which had nothing whatever to do with the issue at hand, took about five minutes. Upon completion, he looked gravely at each member of the board in turn, while he folded the clipping carefully and slipped it into a manila folder in front of him. A moment of silence followed.

I jumped in and repeated my suggestion. It worked. They did it. They passed a murky empowering resolution that would be enough, I thought, to reassure students and faculty that the board meant to be true to the spirit of the agreement.

Timing is all. They were embarrassed that Dr. Lillehammer had appeared so foolish in front of their new president. He probably did this sort of thing often, and they'd gotten used to it. Their support of my position was a consolation prize.

They weren't finished. They'd given me the crumb I wanted. Now they had one for Phil.

"Mr. Chairman," said Stanley Maytag, "the development committee of the board respectfully recommends that a testimonial dinner be held in President Emeritus Harkness's honor, and that the new library be named after him."

"Out of order," Curtis boomed. "I will entertain a motion for adjournment."

"So moved."

Curtis rapped his gavel, and the meeting was over. Nobody was very happy about the outcome, except me. Bruno Altman, from the justice department, had sat through the entire meeting, silent and motionless. I envied his composure.

"I'm sorry our agreement wasn't accepted as written," he told me. "We worked hard on that."

"I'm sorry, too," I said.

"Just call me if you need my help," he said amiably. "We bureaucrats are used to not getting everything we'd like. At least we got all the players to the table, and they weren't there before."

Now, near the end of October, he called me and repeated his offer.

"Thanks," I said. "I will."

"In the spring."

"Okay, in the spring."

~

One late-fall evening, I came upon a spectacular sight as I drove home. Around a curve in the road, in a field of corn stubble, I saw hundreds of migrating sandhill cranes, picking through the remains of the harvest before continuing their flight.

Cranes are big birds with legs like stilts, much taller than herons, whom they most resemble. I was exhilarated by the sight—as though I had come upon a Japanese print in a portfolio of student work. I pulled my car over onto the shoulder of the road and watched them for several minutes. Some of the males were performing stylized dances and jumps, wings spread wide, in front of selected females. I remembered a video I had once seen (*Nature*? *Wild Kingdom*?). In it, an ornithologist donned a crane costume and danced their ancient mating dance in order to arouse the reproductive enthusiasm of an indifferent female. Did it work? I couldn't quite remember.

A few groups of cranes were aloft that evening near sunset, wheeling in wide circles and settling in, out of my sight, on the other side of a hill. When I passed the same field the next morning, they had all vanished. They'd be back in the spring, though, I was sure, like all the migratory birds that were making brief stops in the area.

CHAPTER 5

November: The President's Agenda

Finally. At the homecoming meeting of the Board of Trustees, on Friday, the day before the big football game, I presented a reasonable set of priorities, and I told the board what I thought could be accomplished and what I thought must be accomplished.

The crises and embarrassments that had shaken the college in the spring, and now in the first months of my presidency, added to all our anxieties. Racial peace, even if achieved, would be a hollow victory if Middleton College collapsed, and right now it was very shaky. An act of violence, a fire, a student walkout, could bring it down—and all those events had happened at the college in recent memory.

These are dangerous times for small colleges. A year ago, thirty miles from Middleton, a small college had closed its doors forever. Enrollment problems. The specter was not easily forgotten, especially since Middleton College had enrollment problems, too: numbers of recruited students had declined almost every year, and the retention of recruited students had also gone down.

Now, eighty percent of the students came from the bottom two quartiles of the ACT Assessment, a standardized national admissions test. Only thirty percent of students from other colleges in the region were ranked that low.

Fewer than forty-five percent of entering freshmen at Middleton ever became seniors. The college needed more students, and it needed to stop the enrollment skid right away.

Any agenda we adopted, I believed, would have to benefit everyone in some clearly discernible way.

I worried about white backlash. The resentment I could feel from white students and a few faculty and staff members and their refusal to talk publicly about racial issues were not good signs. From the perspective of a disgruntled few, their little college, which had been too poor to resurface the running track or raise faculty salaries, had found $100,000 for what they regarded as frills. Multiculturalism to them was an expensive joke.

My strategy was to use an enrollment management plan as a lever to move the institution forward. Better use of financial aid dollars and recruitment in new areas should lead to increased enrollment, and increased enrollment would benefit everyone. Such an effort could be combined with a planning process that would involve all constituencies. A planning group could decide how resources should be allocated to help the institution attract and retain more students *and* to develop programmatic responses to multicultural and civil rights issues, including issues of gender and disability as well as race.

A big assignment. Was it doable?

Yes, with some help. I was familiar with the work of Morgan Enrollment Advisors, a consulting firm that specialized in admissions and retention problems in small colleges. Howie Elbert and Lisa Dunn, two of Morgan's partners, had a record of success at other colleges, and they'd done good work for me before.

I'd invited them to make a presentation before the board at this meeting. They knew their stuff and they knew their audience. Slides and transparencies, columns and trend lines, all showed the direction Middleton was going in and what Morgan Enrollment Advisors could do to turn things around.

The board was convinced. Its members voted unanimously

to hire their company, and I set Howie and Lisa to work at once to find any obstacles to Middleton's enrollment success. We needed to remove at least some of the barriers. They knew where to look and how to analyze the data they collected.

The board endorsed my proposed work plan: one-third of my time to be spent on planning; one-third on multicultural and civil rights issues; and one-third on enrollment management. The trustees also endorsed my idea of establishing separate task forces on Greek life, alcohol policy, and judicial processes, because I had discovered life-safety issues—those kerosene heaters in fraternity rooms were only one of them—and issues of equity in the administration of the student judicial system. Those task forces would include students, faculty, and administrative staff members. They'd make recommendations to me after they'd studied the issues.

Clearly the trustees and I were on the same wavelength. We all chatted together at the coffee break, trustees, president, and consultants.

"Call me," I said to Lisa and Howie, "as soon as you've completed the survey and analysis of the academic program. The sooner the better, of course."

~

The next day was homecoming, a time for alumni to return to their college, watch a football game, and have a good time.

Alumni are the natural and, every president hopes, enduring friends of a small college. Their loyalty is critical to its success. They don't expect their alma mater to produce Nobel Prize winners or Rose Bowl champions (although a conference championship is always welcome, and Middleton's loss of a championship was a painful blow). They don't long for new buildings to rise on familiar acreage, and they're tolerant of aging classrooms or a gutted fraternity house.

What they *do* want is to read about their classmates in

the *Alumni News*, mentally measuring themselves against the achievements of their peers, and to see familiar faces when they come to campus for homecoming or class reunions. They want to know that the faculty members they loved are being treated well, and that the president of their college isn't grinding Old Prof down.

On all these matters the alumni of Middleton College had cause for concern, maybe even alarm. The *Alumni News* had not appeared for some time. There was nobody to write it because the public information officer at Middleton had left for greener pastures after the April Incident and hadn't yet been replaced. Consequently the "Class Notes" that many had supplied months before—new jobs, new spouses, new addresses, new children and grandchildren—were growing stale.

Recent graduates who came back to campus might find all their old favorites gone because of the high turnover in the past couple of decades. The faculty who had stayed had suffered two salary cuts over the past ten years. Their teaching loads were unusually heavy. These painful strategies had made it possible to keep tuition low. Nobody had pointed this out explicitly. It would have seemed too manipulative; too, well, too unfamilylike to punish one group in order to ease the burdens on another. But you didn't need to be either a mathematician or a Machiavelli to figure out that's what had been happening.

There was a good turnout of alums who came back to homecoming that year. It was a glorious day. To be quite frank, though, it had an inauspicious beginning for me.

The day began with the twelfth-annual 5-K run from the college campus, past the high school, through the oak woods, and back to the campus, up the hill to the finish line. The "Run for the Acorns," it was called, and the souvenir T-shirt pictured smiling squirrels.

I've been a distance runner for many years, so, in the spirit of the day, I decided to join the run. I fired the starting gun, then jumped into the race, near the last of the seventy-five or so alumni who were participating. When I reached the one-mile mark, the timekeeper called out, "Six minutes and thirty seconds." I laughed. I have seldom run a mile in fewer than eight minutes. Was the timekeeper trying to curry favor with the new president? Never mind.

I plunged into the woods, following the path that soon diverged, unmarked, in two directions. By now I was bringing up the rear. Every runner's nightmare: I've lost the course, and I'm last.

So enjoy the weather, I told myself, ambling now in the general direction of the campus. I emerged, ran along the street in back of the campus, and at last up the hill to the finish line. A few administrators and staff members were there, cheering me wildly. I was grateful to see other humans. The race director read out a preposterously low finishing time.

"I lost my way," I explained, "I couldn't find the course markers."

"Oh I'm sorry," said the race director. "There aren't any. Everybody knows the course."

I drove home to take a shower, and on the way I listened to *Life and Death in Shanghai*, my current book on tape. It helped me put the proper perspective on the morning's hardships. I came back in time for the football game, and though the Wildcats lost, autumn delivered spectacular weather.

Everyone who gathered under the beer tents and around the tailgates after the game had a story to tell me as they shook my hand and smiled toward the official photographer who followed me around. They told me about their undergraduate days at Middleton College because they liked to reminisce, but also because they wanted me to know, and maybe even to love, the college as thoroughly and deeply as they did.

As for the calamities that had put Middleton College in the media spotlight since April, the alumni were remarkably sanguine. "It was blown out of all proportion," one after another confidently assured me about the April Incident and its splashy aftermath.

I saw only one African American alumnus at the postgame festivities. In the 1950s and 1960s, at least, many black students had attended Middleton College. Two from the class of 1949 were on the Board of Trustees. One of them, Ernest Newman, a successful public-school administrator, was fond of reminiscing about the total acceptance he had found at Middleton College. At the trustees' meeting I had heard him speak with gratitude and conviction about racial integration as he had known it then. Apparently integration had worked for him. The fact that he was the only black face I saw at homecoming, except on the football field, suggested that it hadn't worked for many others.

~

Homecoming had reminded me how much we—I—needed a director of public information. To have that post vacant meant that there was no one to publicize good things about the college and no one to assure that on-campus communications were going well. I was spending far too many precious hours in front of cameras or composing memos. Matt Austin was doing an effective job as our PR consultant, and I trusted his advice, but he couldn't give interviews or turn out the weekly informational memos that the on-campus community required, or the press releases that needed to be sent to all the media on a regular basis. Although a director of sports information had survived the April Incident, he had neither the skills nor the interest in taking on a larger assignment.

The development office was directing the recruitment of a new director, because that person would report to the development vice president. But because I knew that person would have to work closely with me, I interviewed the three finalists for the position. One, Rhoda Dillard, an African American who had worked in higher education for several years, was outstanding. I recommended to the search committee that she be hired.

If you are accustomed to the hiring practices of corporate, for-profit organizations, the ways of higher education will seem strange and cumbersome. They are. A search committee is formed to fill nearly every professional or faculty position. First it composes the job description; then it advertises the job, and it sets a deadline for receiving applications. When a pool of resumes has accumulated, the search committee begins calling references and culling the group. Three or four qualified candidates are brought to campus. At a small college like Middleton, each candidate may meet only with the search committee, or with the search committee and the president, or with different groups on campus who then report their opinions to the search committee by filling out evaluation forms.

As you can see, the process is slow, especially because the task of interviewing and hiring is added to the regular job responsibilities of members of the search committee. Colleges usually have a personnel officer who helps with the paperwork, but the tasks of evaluation and judgment are left to those who have no particular expertise in such matters.

Thirty years ago, this cumbersome process didn't exist. College presidents or vice presidents called their friends at other colleges and asked for the names of promising candidates for one position or another. The academic dean or perhaps the appropriate department head called friends who were graduate trainers to recommend promising students. This was what is now familiarly called the old boys' network. In a few days, a suitable person could be found and interviewed. Most turned out to be white and male.

The new system, now some thirty years old, was designed

to diversify the workforce in higher education, and to a significant extent it has succeeded. The faculty and administrative positions I had held, for example, would not even have been *known* to me a generation ago. I thanked the civil rights movement for my opportunities. Begun as a drive for racial justice and equality, it had given rise to an equally powerful movement to end gender inequalities. Affirmative action was mandated in the Civil Rights Act of 1964 and expanded to include women in the amendments of 1972. The hiring process that emerged, being a human invention, was flawed. It took precious time, and it took power away from the administrative leadership of a college. Some people didn't like that. Also, the old boys' networks sometimes still worked, but in subtler ways, and some women and some members of minority groups believed that times were better when discrimination was out in the open.

I didn't agree, and I was not troubled by new imperfections. As for the hiring at hand, I liked Rhoda Dillard. So did the search committee. Rhoda liked us well enough to accept the job, and she started work in mid-November.

Rhoda was an attractive, confident woman in her mid-forties with a personality of great warmth and good humor. Her grandparents had brought their children north during World War II, when jobs opened up for "Negroes" in the steel mills. Her father had earned a good living in the mills, and his children went to college, the first generation in their family to do so. Grandpa had died many years ago, but Grandma still called her children, and some of her grandchildren, every evening.

Rhoda and her husband lived in Echo River, twenty miles from Middleton. Their four children were in college or out of school and working, but Rhoda and John had recently adopted Paul, a five-year-old who lived in their neighborhood. Paul had started wandering over to the Dillards at mealtimes and began staying longer and longer, asking to watch television with Rhoda and John, asking if they had drawing paper and crayons he could use, finally asking if he could stay all night. After a few months, the Dillards talked with Paul's mother, and they all agreed that adoption would be in everybody's best interest.

I learned that part much later, but when she was interviewing for the position Rhoda had told us that she had a five-year-old. "I might be absent for a day now and then, if Paul gets sick. John and I trade off for those times, but when it's my turn, it's my turn. Unless there's a critical emergency here at the college."

"No problem," I assured her. A generation ago, no job candidate, especially not a woman, would have admitted to child-care responsibilities that might occasionally require attention during business hours.

Rhoda knew what Middleton College needed in the way of communications, and she was prepared to provide it. She had both the skills and the savvy. She had other qualities that we needed. The African American students liked her at once. Many of them found their way, one by one, to her office, and she always took time to chat with them. This, after all, was communication, too.

Rhoda was a black professional in a white world, and she was an effective bridge across the color line. How was she able to do that, I wondered, without being hopelessly torn or angry? She knew that people on the street in Middleton stopped and watched her as she drove her Oldsmobile up Main Street to the campus. After she became a more familiar sight, she smiled and waved to them, and they waved back.

I was always glad to see her when she came to my office—something she did often. In an environment of frequent crises, she needed to know what I was thinking and doing, so she was not blindsided, and I needed to know how the media might interpret whatever they thought I was thinking and doing. She helped me understand the African American students as individuals, because they revealed themselves to her more authentically than they ever would to me.

My pleasure in having her at Middleton, however, went far beyond her interpretive skills or her ability to relate to the African American students. She was a woman, and I saw very few in my daily course of administrative business. Alice Peterson, the director of development, was another—a welcome sight, for reasons I couldn't really name even to myself, except to say she was a woman.

The feeling I had was far more complicated than "letting my hair down," because I never did. That was a luxury I couldn't afford. But I *could* feel myself smile and relax at least a little when either one of them telephoned me or when I saw their names in my appointment book.

Rhoda and I talked often in those early weeks, about the town and how we could repair Middleton College's relations with Middleton. Some town-gown conflict occurs wherever there's a college, but there hadn't been much in Middleton until the April Incident. The movers and shakers in town had truly liked Phil Harkness, and they liked what they knew of Middleton College: it brought football to town on many an autumnal Saturday; it provided jobs, poorly paid, but jobs nonetheless, to Middleton citizens. It opened its gyms to the schoolkids of the village, and its meeting rooms to the Rotary and Kiwanis. It mostly improved the quality of life in the village.

Oh sure, the students had wild parties in their fraternity houses—Chief Janowicz and Officer Beasley were often called to break things up and send people off to bed—but the parties and their aftermaths, real and imagined, provided good conversation at the Edgewood Inn. College life was like this.

The good feeling had protected Middleton College in earlier

crises. Three years before the April Incident, an African American student had been stabbed and badly wounded by a recent graduate at a fraternity party. The alum, a white man, had died in an automobile accident two hours later, on his way home. Because the stabbing had taken place off campus and not at a college event, the president had successfully referred all calls to the Middleton police.

In the same year, thousands of dollars' worth of college property had been stolen from buildings that were protected only by student workers acting as security guards. And shortly after the renovation and expansion of the library had begun, that wall had collapsed while students and workers were inside. None of those events had achieved much notice beyond the village.

The April Incident was different. Instantly it had leaped beyond the village boundaries. Strangers with cameras and notepads came to town, and some of the local merchants believed that the reporters had already cast them as rednecks and bigots. One reporter had discovered that the nearby town of Fremont had once been a center of KKK activity. What did that have to do with anything? people had asked. Soon the locals were refusing to give any interviews.

The era of good feeling ended when Phil Harkness retired.

We needed to restore the trust and pride that the town had once taken in its college. Rhoda needed to become a familiar presence in town, and to become trusted as a spokesperson for the college.

That would take a long time, but we could make a start. We began having lunch at the Edgewood Inn about once a week, and very soon Rhoda knew all the regulars. She occasionally went there with one or two of the African American students.

Next we worked on improving relations with Chief Janowicz. I invited him to have breakfast with Rhoda and me in my office one morning so we could all become better acquainted on an ordinary, crisis-free day. It was a first for me. I'd never had breakfast with someone who wore a revolver to the table. Walt (we agreed to call one another by our first names) was more amiable than the last time he was here, after the theft of the financial aid checks. I wondered how often he and Phil had gotten together, and I wondered what they had talked about.

"We'd rather be called sooner than later," said Walt, as we discussed law enforcement, "if the college has a problem that's getting out of hand, or a party that's out of control. We won't ignore underage drinking, but kids'll be safer if they do it inside.

"We don't discriminate by race, either," he continued. "Black or white, they're all the same to us. Our job is to enforce the law, and that's what we do." Rhoda looked dubious. I thought about Tyrone being stopped for a broken taillight, and Bryant cooling his heels for hours at the police station. "I try to stay away from the media," he said, "but I can't keep things off the police records."

"Of course not." Rhoda and I nodded.

"I don't give interviews. I've got some ideas, though, about how you can tighten up security here—so you don't have any more thefts, things like that."

"I'll ask Art Dove to call you about that," I suggested.

We finished our juice and muffins.

"Nice to meet you," he said to Rhoda as he pushed back his chair, brushed away a few crumbs, and laid his napkin on the small, round table.

We all smiled warmly.

~

Rhoda needed to know the faculty, too. She wanted to develop a small biographical sketch on each one for her files—

what each member's specialty was, what memberships they held—so she could encourage the media to call on them for feature stories or for comment on news that touched their areas of expertise. Faculty are always at their best when they're talking about what they love, and they would welcome being consulted on matters other than race relations.

A good project, but one that would take time. I was still getting acquainted myself with members of the faculty. Some were rarely seen outside their classrooms. Ted Lynskey in biology, for instance. He had come to that first open meeting I'd had in August and told me about the changes he'd experienced in the twenty-five years he'd been at Middleton: his labs were old-fashioned and the instrumentation out-of-date. His students, he thought, were not nearly as good as they'd been a generation ago. He cheered himself by collecting butterflies and moths and serving as regional coordinator for the annual National Butterfly Census. Even this was not an unclouded source of pleasure: he told me there were fewer varieties in the region each year, and fewer within each variety. I scarcely saw Ted after that first meeting.

I saw some faculty members frequently, at lunch. There was no separate faculty dining room or faculty club at Middleton, so most days, if I wasn't dining at the Edgewood Inn or speaking at a Rotary Club, or meeting with an anxious parent or alum, I took my tray through the cafeteria line, smiled and nodded to the large perspiring women at the steam tables, continued to the salad bar, following nubile young women who looked as if they didn't eat anything that wasn't leafy, drew a Diet Coke from the soda machine, then chose a seat at one of the long tables where members of the faculty sat. Often Rhoda Dillard came with me. Occasionally a couple of students braved a faculty table and joined us. Black students almost never did. They sat together at the far end of the dining hall, often with Bryant Dunbar. This kind of self-segregation was troubling to white people. Someone almost invariably called it to my attention. The president of another small college in the state told me he didn't permit it. "If you want to go to school here, you mix with everybody. I tell them that the first day."

I liked the faculty members whom I came to know over lunch. They came from more varied backgrounds than faculty I had known at other colleges: Louise Holmberg taught biology, but she had been trained as a veterinarian and had worked in a pet clinic. After a few years, she left her practice for a job at Middleton College.

"You were bored working with animals?" I asked.

"No. I loved the animals. It was the owners. I got angry with the owners. I hated the holiday season: that's when we had a huge upsurge in euthanasia business."

"Why?" So much for beloved pets.

"Different reasons. People wanted to spruce up their homes for Christmas and didn't want an old dog around to smell up the place; or they wanted to get a puppy, so they got rid of the grown-up dog; or they wanted a different breed. For many of my clients, taking a pet to be put down was like taking old clothes to the Goodwill.

"When I realized I was angry all the time, I knew I had to do something else. I love teaching here. I was lucky to get the job." Her gratitude and her unconventional background were, perhaps, the reasons her salary was so low. I'd reviewed the salary schedule when I first came to Middleton. Salaries were all over the map. Well, not *all* over. The southern hemisphere only. It looked to me as if you received what you could negotiate. There weren't any salary ranges for various ranks. I hadn't looked for gender discrimination in the salaries because I didn't have time to do the analysis, and the records I needed weren't all in the same place.

Jim Black taught part-time in the business department—

courses in its flagship concentration, real estate. Jim was the first person I ever met from Middleton College. He'd picked me up at the hotel the day I came to campus for an interview. He had a cheerful, outgoing manner, and he liked Middleton College. He'd retired early from a government job with HUD. Now he was around young people three days a week, and he wasn't being smothered by a huge bureaucracy.

"The kids are great," he had said as he drove me to campus that summer day, "and I'm crazy about teaching. The two years I've been at the college have been the best of my life."

Jim's colleagues in the department—they sat together at lunch—weren't as enthusiastic as he, but, like Jim, they enjoyed what they were doing. Dave Charnley, who was also in the business department, was a graduate of Middleton College, now finishing his Ph.D. at the state university. He didn't think the April Incident was some aberrant storm in a sea of racial tranquillity. In fact, shortly after the incident he had given an interview to a reporter from a big-city newspaper: "I had an African American roommate when I was a student here five years ago," he was quoted as saying. (Charnley is white.) "We got death threats on the telephone."

Did that really happen? I wondered. Why else would he say it?

There was a bravado about that interview, a bravado shared by other members of the business department, not visible in their colleagues from other disciplines. Perhaps they felt less trapped than the professors in the humanities, and less responsible for solving Middleton's ills than faculty in the social sciences. The business faculty could go back to the business world if all else failed. They liked this life better, except for the low salaries, but they had other choices or believed they did.

Another factor no doubt contributing to their bold spirits (at least until it was time to read papers and grade examinations) was that their classes were overflowing. Business administration was by far the largest major at the college—as it is at many other small colleges, including some of the best ones. Students wanted to be in their classes, because they were convinced that some form of business was the key to a secure future.

Lucas and Jill Henderson, both sociologists, were almost always in the dining hall when I was there. Lucas spent time with some of the African American students. Donald Thomas, one of the black leaders who had emerged in April, was a sociology major, and he occasionally touched base with Lucas at lunch.

"He's a very interesting young man," Lucas told me after one of Donald's visits. "Last year, before April, when some of the African American seniors were beginning to feel they'd been cheated here, hadn't been listened to, Donald wouldn't have anything to do with them. In fact, he went out of his way to let me and his other professors know he was not part of that group.

"He stuck with the white students, even thought about joining one of the fraternities, really belonging, you know? I think the April Incident changed him. But even then he wasn't one of the black students who left the campus. He stayed around, finished the semester, but told the press he'd been deeply hurt by what had happened. 'They don't want us here,' he'd said. I think that was a terrible discovery for him."

~

Less than a month after homecoming, long after a strong wind had taken down the leafy arcades over the campus streets and left only the dark architecture of tree limbs, and when the piles of building material outside the library-in-progress had begun to look less promising than they had when flowers bloomed and grass grew, Lisa Dunn called me. "I've finished the analysis of the academic program, as you and the board asked," she said. "We need to talk. Off campus would probably be best."

CHAPTER 6

December: Holidays and Hard Choices

From the breathy confidential tone of Lisa's voice over the telephone, I felt as if I were part of the Manhattan Project, and nothing less significant than splitting the atom would be revealed to me when we met. Consultants are sometimes like that.

She did get my attention. We met the next evening for supper at the Olde English Pub & Carriage House in Jefferson Mills.

"We have some pretty serious problems here," she said after we'd ordered two Pub-burgers and coleslaw, and two glasses of mineral water.

"They're definitely problems that interfere with your ability to attract and retain students. They're going to be noticed by that accreditation team that's coming year after next.

"I'll leave you my entire report," she continued, "and you can decide what to do with it. Ready for the summary?"

"Let's have it."

"In a nutshell, the academic program has been running on empty for quite a while, and sometimes the college has provided false information about the program to its accrediting bodies. The last North Central accrediting team made a note of that, without comment.

"The college doesn't follow its own admissions requirements. You have kids who've never taken the ACT, which all your admissions materials say prospectives must take, and I found one student who it looks like didn't graduate from high school and didn't take the GED either. He plays football, and if the league ever finds out about him, your teams could be put on probation until the millennium. Not to mention that the media will have another feeding frenzy at Middleton's expense.

"Then there's all these courses that are in the catalog. About twenty percent of them haven't been taught for three years or more.

"You have almost no faculty advisement of students either. You have something called peer advising. I don't think the accreditation people would approve, and I don't think it meets students' expectations either. It's certainly not the 'close student-faculty interaction' that the admissions brochures promise.

"You have quite a few remedial courses, you know, and they're really essential, given the low achievement scores of many students. But they're being taught by instructors who have no college teaching experience or training for remedial work."

Petosky had noted that in his report, too.

"You have one faculty member whose only previous experience was teaching the eighth grade in one of the little towns around here, Fremont, I think." (Was she the teacher, I wondered, who had been writing on the blackboard when the alleged incident of penis-wagging occurred?)

Lisa continued. "Many of the faculty are teaching *way* out of their fields, because of the core program for one thing, and that's not going to change anytime soon. The faculty has committed itself to teaching a whole flock of new courses in African American studies. The dean plans to hire part-timers to cover some of them. If he does, that sends the percentage of part-time faculty way up past what's normally tolerable.

"And you already know that there aren't any clear standards for hiring or compensation or promotion of faculty," Lisa concluded.

We ate and drank in silence for a while.

"I need a dessert," I said.

Lisa nodded. When we'd finished, she handed me her report.

"There's much more in here," she said. "It's all thoroughly documented. I have the numbers on everything. It's no wonder you have a hard time getting students and keeping the ones you do get. You're pretty close to going out of business. But we can fix a lot of it this year, if we make the right moves."

We paid the check, and left the pub.

"The chair of the Board of Trustees needs to hear this first," I said as we shook hands and parted. "Then we can decide what to do with it next. We should wait until after Thanksgiving, though."

"If it would be helpful for me to make some kind of general presentation," Lisa said, "I'll do it. Just give me a few days' notice."

Lisa gathered her fur coat around her (admissions consulting for small colleges is well-compensated work), slid into her rented car, and headed for the airport. I walked home down the main street of Jefferson Mills. Christmas lights had already been strung across the street. Local shops were cheerily decorated for the holidays. Blinking red lights and a beckoning plastic Santa decorated Tony's Newsstand and Smoke Shop, which had the largest inventory of biker porn I'd ever seen. The cover of each magazine showed some variation of a sultry young woman thrusting her leather-clad pelvis toward the viewer or toward a motorcycle. An O-gauge electric train circled the "Gifts for the Handyman" display in the window of Mills Hardware ("Open till Eight for Your Holiday Convenience").

My mind drifted back many years. My father owned and operated a jewelry store in Minneapolis when I was a girl. Every year, on the Sunday just after Thanksgiving, he would go downtown to the store to decorate the windows for the holidays, and I often went along. His decorations were simple: artfully draped white satin, a few pieces of elegant jewelry, and some Christmas tree decorations and lights he'd brought when he emigrated from Germany long ago. One year the Bulova Corporation sent all its dealers an illuminated Santa for holiday display, but we took it home and hung it outside.

I mostly wandered around the store, trying on jewelry and winding watches, popping the spring tops of empty ring boxes. At noon my job was to walk two blocks down Third Street to Charlie's Chicken Shack and buy our carryout lunch. Dad's store was not in the high-rent district, and the walk scared me. Vagrant old men struggling with hangovers, wearing threadbare overcoats and unbuckled galoshes, hung around Charlie's, which was right next door to the Salvation Army Hospitality Center.

"Just tend to your own business," my father advised, when I confessed to being frightened, "and you'll be fine." Fear was not an acceptable emotion. (I was afraid now. Afraid that the college could crumble before my eyes, maybe next weekend.) I construed his words to mean that my eyes must be rigidly directed forward and I must look neither to the left nor to the right as I marched purposefully to Charlie's. Dad was right. No harm or even the hint of harm ever came to me. The trip was just scary enough, though, to give me an exciting tingle of danger and then a glow of pride in danger overcome.

The streets of Jefferson Mills were anything but scary, unless you find Victorian architecture intimidating—echoes of the Addams family, perhaps. The town was devoted to preserving its nineteenth-century ambience. One hundred years ago it had been a prosperous commercial center, served by a now-long-vanished railroad. The homes and shops and some of the prosperity from those days were still here. Residential streets were lined with Victorian homes, large and small, and gardens to match. Many of the buildings were on the National Register of Historic Places.

Every September, Jefferson Mills sponsored a tour of its historic homes. Five or six of the Victorian beauties, different ones each year, were opened to the public. Tour buses from Chicago and Milwaukee and even Des Moines brought thousands of visitors on Home Tour Weekend. Local and imported talent provided daylong entertainment on the lawns of the designated homes: at one, a barbershop quartet held forth; at another, a young harpist in a diaphanous gown that swirled in the slightest breeze; and at still a third, a fading tenor singing old favorites—"Just before the Battle, Mother," "I'll Take You Home Again Kathleen." The churches served lunch and dinner, all good, wholesome fare, prepared by the town's best cooks. I'd stolen a few Saturday hours to make the tour and sample the cooking. Delightful! Visions of a bygone era, as the brochures and posters promised.

Another town festival would soon be here. To celebrate Christmas and stimulate holiday business, the town held its Festival of Light on the first weekend in December. As night fell on that Saturday and Sunday afternoon, the combined choirs from all the local churches, each member holding a wavering candle, sang carols in the town square, and lights were turned on, all up and down the streets of Jefferson Mills, bright spokes fanning out from the flickering hub. Each year, I was told, more and more people decorated their homes and yards. Santa and reindeer, manger scenes, and Frosty the Snowman. Each year, preparations began a little earlier—hence Main Street already glowing, well before Thanksgiving.

Jefferson Mills, population ten thousand, was considered a very desirable community in which to live. The public schools were good, crime and violence were low, and civic pride was high.

The town's resident population was entirely white. Everybody knew that. Nobody mentioned it. Although two large insurance companies had their headquarters in Jefferson Mills, and many black professionals worked there, they were steered away from buying homes in town. "You'd be happier in Echo River," real estate agents explained. "There's an interesting variety of people there." A woman I came to know, who was a vice president at Provident Home Insurance in Jefferson Mills, had resigned from the local planning commission because, she told me, she was so tired of hearing the phrase "safe growth," the watchword of town planning.

During Home Tour Weekend, Arnie Anthony and his wife, Charlene, both new faculty members at Middleton College and both African American, had moved into a rental condominium in a new development on the outskirts of town. The first night they were in Jefferson Mills, the back window of their Honda was smashed while they were in the Olde English Pub having dinner.

"Just some crazy people," Arnie said mildly when I asked him about it. "Probably from out of town. Probably drunk. I'll bet we won't have any more trouble. They've probably gone back where they came from."

There hadn't been any more trouble, and Arnie told me his neighbors were warm and friendly. They agreed with him that the damage must have been done by teenagers from out of town.

Snowflakes began to fall as I turned up Ashmore Drive to my non-Victorian, split-level house. By the time I went out for my three-mile run the next morning, snow had blanketed everything in a soothing whiteness. Tony had shoveled the walk in front of his Newsstand and Smoke Shop by the time I stopped in to pick up my morning paper.

~

For the next couple of weeks I struggled with what to do with what I knew. The Board of Trustees had been struggling for the past year, and with far less information than I now had. Some of them had sensed that the college wasn't like other small colleges, and their president and his deans weren't telling them all that they needed to know. That's why they had hired the consultant, Gerald Petosky, to examine the entire college; that's why they had asked Phil Harkness to retire and why they had endorsed the broad agenda I'd proposed in October. Did the two deans, Harlan Elliot and Bonnie Truesdell, need to go, too?

I'd been thinking about that since the day I took office, and now I had Lisa's analysis to add to what I'd known before. If I let Harlan and Bonnie go, I'd need to find interim deans to serve until a new president arrived. They couldn't just be placeholders either, any more than I was. The dean of students needed to be someone who could take hold of the campus and not be intimidated by either the athletic establishment or the Greeks. The academic dean had to be a person who could direct strategic planning, earn the faculty's trust and cooperation, overnight if possible, and begin directing changes in the academic program.

If I let the deans go, there would be a ruckus—more than there would be if I were a man. In the past twenty years, women presidents have become familiar in higher education; in 1992, we comprised eleven percent of all college and university presidents. When a woman is hired, she is seldom a curiosity anymore. But when she visibly exercises the power of her office, when she gives or takes away money or jobs, she suddenly reminds people that she is not the queen of England or Miss America, neither a figurehead nor a popular icon. Then many of her erstwhile admirers ask themselves anew whether it is a good idea to have a woman in such a position of authority.

The trustees were still divided among themselves over what

had happened since the April before. I took heart from their unanimous vote to hire Morgan Enrollment Advisors as consultants, because one of my goals was to find projects around which everyone could rally in support of a stronger Middleton College, and this first test had done just that.

But on the day when they'd accepted the enrollment plan in the morning, they'd dropped Curtis Havel as board chair in the afternoon. Evelyn Hart, an able, intelligent woman who had served on the board for several years, had emerged as the victorious candidate. She turned out to be the best board chair I ever worked with, thoroughly committed to the well-being of Middleton College. Not long after her appointment, though, one of the senior members of the board was quoted as saying to another, with dismay, "Two women are running our college."

Some trustees thought that would be the end of strife and the end of change. Wishful thinking. If a new president were to be successful—and a search committee had already been formed and applications were being received—he or she could not begin by terminating two deans. That would use up too much of the new president's reservoir of goodwill. Clearing the deck, if indeed the deck had to be cleared, was my job. That was one reason why an interim president had been brought in from outside, and why she agreed *not* to be a candidate for the long-term job.

I thought, with a twinge of longing, of how different it was in federal and state politics. When a new president or governor takes office, he or she is likely to be of a different political party than the incumbent. That being so, everyone from the old administration expects to get the heave-ho from the new. Not so in higher education.

In large universities, the central administrators know that they serve at the pleasure of the president and that they may be removed from their positions if the chief executive officer so desires. Usually, however, they have "tenure homes" to return to, academic departments to which they are tenured as faculty members and where they may earn their (much-reduced) keep by teaching.

In small colleges, the fate of administrators is less certain. At Middleton College, which had no tenure system, there was no guaranteed place for an unwanted administrator to go, except to another job at another college.

Early in November I had spoken confidentially to Bryant Dunbar, the administrator whose credentials made him the logical choice to serve as acting dean of students.

"I may have to make a change," I said. "Would you be willing to take on the job? It wouldn't be easy. You would need to take control of some little fiefdoms that have had their own way for years, and you'd have to lean on quite a few people to make sure they carry out the recommendations of the task forces I've appointed."

Bryant nodded quickly. "Of course. I'm sorry if that has to happen, but I wouldn't have any hesitation about taking on the job. I know I could do it. No problem."

"I'd need to get someone to fill in for you as director of multicultural services for about six months. I'd guarantee that you could return to your old job then."

"If you do decide to make the change," Bryant said, "I've got an idea who could do multicultural services for a semester. A friend of mine. Bob Brown. He's a graduate student in African American studies, A.B.D. [all doctoral work completed but the dissertation] at the state university, but he's older than the usual graduate student. He was in the marines for a long time, as an embassy guard somewhere in Africa—Ghana, I think, or Guinea. I'll have him send you his resume."

"Not yet," I said. "Let's wait until I'm sure there's a job he might apply for."

Replacing the academic dean would be more difficult. Lisa

Dunn had suggested a faculty member from the business school at one of the SUNY (State University of New York) campuses, Greg Davidson.

"He's done short-term work for Howie and me at a couple of colleges. He's bored where he is, and his home campus would probably be delighted to give him a semester's unpaid leave. It would ease their budget.

"He's good, and he's a bleeding heart, too," she had told me. "He'd be interested in a place that's trying to grapple with racial issues. I'll mention the possibility to him."

"Not yet."

The timing was important. I couldn't terminate the two deans until the end of the semester, but I had to do it then, in order to give Bonnie and Harlan as much time as possible to find other jobs and to give their replacements a full semester to launch the enrollment and planning efforts. This meant letting them go a week before Christmas. I needed to announce their replacements at the same time I announced their departure, and I had to make sure that the trustees knew exactly when this was to happen at least a whisper before everyone else did. Before any of that, I'd have to talk to Evelyn Hart about the appropriate severance package for both deans. I wanted to be sure they received full compensation at least through commencement, and that was more generous than had been President Harkness's custom.

Rhoda needed to know enough in advance that she could prepare press releases and schedule a press conference. The media would love this one: Mrs. Scrooge fires the Crachits.

~

Thanksgiving has almost always been my favorite holiday. When I was a child, I liked it because it marked the beginning of a season of excitement and anticipation. When I was a young mother, I liked it because family expectations were simple and easy to meet—a good meal served in a festive spirit—and the holiday and hence my responsibilities occurred on the first day of a short vacation.

For the previous ten years Thanksgiving had been my favorite because I flew off to New Jersey (usually on Thursday morning, to avoid the airport crush of Wednesday night) to spend the holiday with my brother and his family, Karl, Judy, and son Peter, in Somerset. I'd started going there when my daughter, Betsy, was in college at Swarthmore. She'd take the train up from Philadelphia, and we'd meet at Karl and Judy's. Now she was in graduate school in Los Angeles, too far to come. In recent years my son, David, had made the trip from his home in St. Paul. All I had to do was to show up by dinnertime.

This year I was inordinately thankful for Thanksgiving. The previous week had been awful. It might have turned into a November Incident, the sort of thing I feared most. Students had begun celebrating on Monday night. The sequence of events was murky, but the recipe was familiar, booze the key ingredient. The outcome, thank God, was relatively benign: no physical injuries, no headlines.

The local police had been called to the campus twice during the night, either by the Security Incs. or by the RAs in one of the residence halls. Loud music, louder and louder voices, rowdy noisy kids throwing beer at each other on the campus quad. When Officer Beasley arrived, they started throwing beer at him. This probably didn't improve his state of mind, but they quieted down in a while, and he left. After the second call, Officer Beasley requested assistance from the Fremont village police. "They're getting pretty rowdy," he radioed.

By 3:00 a.m. about fifty students were milling around the quadrangle yelling at each other—"fucking nigger" was reported though it was unclear whether a white or a black person had yelled it. Two black students banged on the door of the women's residence hall, and when nobody let them in, they broke the locks and entered. Somebody broke a window. A very drunk, very frightened young woman was crying hysterically inside.

When Beasley returned with reinforcements, at about the same time Bonnie Truesdell, the dean of students, arrived—one of the RAs had probably called her, or maybe Beasley did—he yelled at Bonnie, "The campus is out of control."

I learned this much from Bonnie and Beasley and then from Chief Janowicz when they talked to me the next day about what had happened.

"We're getting pretty sick of this," Janowicz told me on Tuesday when he returned from deer hunting. "You've had three false fire alarms this fall. Then there was the explosion in the toilet—something somebody stole from the chem lab—and the marijuana dealer who was also a thief, and I don't know how many drunk and disorderly calls. My officers are tired. Worse yet, they're insulted every time they come up there."

"Is this worse than other years just before Thanksgiving?" I asked.

"You bet it is," he replied.

Was that really true? And if it was true, why was it happening? "I don't think race had much to do with it," Beasley told me when he called my office on Tuesday to explain what he thought had happened. "Even though there was some name calling."

Tuesday night had been calm. Many students had already left campus by then, and by Wednesday noon the campus was deserted. (I reflected on the draconian practices of my college days, when early absence for a vacation period brought swift and sure punishment, outlined clearly in the student handbook: the offending student would be "campused" for ten days. Who would obey such a sentence today, even if it were imposed? Leaving early was the college equivalent of gum chewing in high school: offenses that had been obsolete since the 1960s.)

Early Thursday, I drove to the airport, boarded the plane, and settled back for a quiet flight. As the plane circled Newark for landing, on a perfectly clear morning, I looked out the window and imagined the tens of thousands of turkeys roasting in the tens of thousands of little houses below. During the next four days, I tried to think of nothing more complicated than that.

The turkey at Karl and Judy's made its contribution to our holiday pleasure, somewhere between the champagne toast and the pumpkin chiffon pie. Late in the evening we pillaged scraps from its ruined carcass and washed them down with wine from a box. We'd drunk the good stuff much earlier.

The next day we all drove over to Princeton, to walk around the campus and do a little Christmas shopping on Nassau Street. As we lunched at the Princeton Inn, I thought enviously about the resources that a rich old university like Princeton could bring to healing race and gender conflict.

Were they doing better than we were at Middleton College?

When Princeton had decided to become coeducational, back in 1969, the alumni had fought like, well, like tigers, to prevent the change. One of the most brutally direct objections was that women graduates would not be able to support Princeton University as men traditionally had, because women didn't earn large salaries, and they weren't as likely as men were to be the custodians of great family wealth.

What about minorities? How welcome were they? How good a place was Princeton for them? Certainly no Princetonian would have said, out loud, that black alumni's modest earning power would stunt the university, but it was surely just as true or as false. I didn't know it then, but a survey on racial climate had just been completed, and ten days after our visit, the *Princeton Alumni Weekly* published the results of the survey, "Racism in Tigertown." The article concluded that racism was a serious problem at Princeton.

Until recent years, surveys of racial attitudes in America

showed that education had a positive effect on attitudes toward race: college-educated citizens were likely to be less prejudiced toward blacks and other minorities than people with no college. Not anymore. In fact, the first racist incidents of the post-civil-rights era had come from one of the elite universities, from Dartmouth. Why? Less economic opportunity for WASPs than before? Too much "special treatment" of minorities? Black separatism?

I mused about all this to myself, over my Caesar salad, while conversation about other subjects swirled around me at the table.

After lunch we spent an hour in the bookstore. The university bookstore nearest to Middleton College was thirty miles away, and I had been missing the familiar activity of browsing.

The rest of the holiday weekend passed in a mellow haze of good conversation, baroque CDs, and rented movies. I remember dozing through a football game on television sometime on Saturday or Sunday.

~

Middleton College's problems didn't seem so formidable when I returned. The snow had melted and a raw wind blew on Monday morning, but Charlie and his grounds crew had done their best to generate a holiday spirit. They had already put up wreaths and Christmas trees in several of the administrative offices and in the lobbies of the residence halls. The faculty Christmas tree was in the dean's office, and everyone, including me, contributed an ornament or two. My tree was a small tabletop model with lights and candy canes.

I had started a new tradition: between 4:00 and 5:00 p.m. every day, the president's office would serve wassail—everybody was invited. Generally a smattering of faculty and staff members dropped in, and even a student or two. Bill Solomon from the business department came every day, unfailingly cheerful.

Geri Schmidt, interim athletic director, came by once or twice. She, too, looked remarkably cheerful. Her appointment hadn't pleased everybody.

"How are things?" I asked her.

"Well, a few of the guys just don't want to do what I say they have to, and I don't think Coach Lombardino is ever going to like having a woman boss. But most people are just fine with it."

True or not, I was glad she had the pizzazz to tell me so. Clearly, she was not being broken by the assignment.

Louise Holmberg from the biology department came to the wassail hour several times, and once she brought a student with her.

"I'd like you to meet Joseph Cabot," she said. We shook hands. "Joe's a senior, and a terrific student. He's already been accepted into a graduate program in environmental science. Last summer he worked for the feds in Alaska. Very interesting work. Salmon, wasn't it, Joe?"

Joe, a tall, thin young man in blue jeans and a Middleton T-shirt, blushed appropriately. "Yes, salmon."

I'd already heard about Joe. He'd grown up on a farm about fifty miles away, and he was one of the ablest students at Middleton College—the sort of student that every professor wants to claim a part of: "He took my English class"; "He did excellent work in my junior core"; "He is an outstanding member of my chamber choir."

He was going to tell me more about the summer project, I could see that, but before he could he was clapped on the shoulder by another of his faculty admirers, and with a polite wave to me he turned away.

A week after Thanksgiving, I asked Lisa Dunn to come back to Middleton and meet with me and Evelyn Hart, to tell her what she had told me about the faults in the academic program. She spread her columns of figures before Evelyn. She opened her copy of the college catalog so that Evelyn could see it. Beside each course was a notation on which year it had last been taught and who had taught it. She laid out lists of students' high school records and ACT scores, and then their college grades.

"Nationally, most college students earn grades that are about one full letter below what they earned in high school. Your students are given grades that average one full letter *higher.* You've got grade inflation like I've never seen."

I remembered a story that a faculty member told me at our open meeting in August. He'd said that when faculty members complained about declining enrollments, Phil Harkness had told them it was their fault—they flunked too many kids. This recollection may not have been true, but if it was, the faculty must have gotten the message.

Evelyn closed her eyes and shook her head.

"There's so much the board hasn't known," she said after a long sigh. "Maybe we didn't ask the right questions. Can we do something about this?" she asked, turning to me.

"Sure. We can get started on it. I think we need to share all this with the faculty, at the beginning of the second semester. By the time we do, we'll have some thoughts about what's the best way to proceed."

Lisa left the meeting so that Evelyn and I could discuss other issues. I told her my plans for replacing the two deans and when I intended to make the change. We agreed on the settlement package for each and the salaries for their replacements.

I still hadn't met Greg Davidson, whom I hoped to put in place immediately after the terminations. We'd talked on the phone a time or two, and I was confident that we were on the same wavelength and that he understood what needed to be done. But I couldn't hire someone sight unseen.

Greg visited the campus on the day of the annual all-campus Christmas party. I liked him at once. He was about forty-five years old, with a firm step and a confident manner. He'd spent much of his career in a highly bureaucratic university. I guessed that he was attracted to this temporary job because there weren't layers of bureaucracy to struggle through. He could make a difference in a short time.

I got right to the point: "First of all I need to have someone look at all the files, all the handbooks governing faculty hiring and promotion, every governing document on curriculum change, everything that concerns record keeping. I'd like you to see whether what we do corresponds to what we say we do.

"I've pretty much decided to present Lisa's report to the faculty at their January meeting. As I see it, that can provide the catalyst for some really significant strategic planning, TQM [total quality management], continuous improvement, whatever. And I'd like representatives from all campus groups to be involved. Can you manage that?" I asked.

"That's my specialty, really." Then he hesitated a moment. "You're not looking to *reduce* the faculty on the basis of this planning effort are you? That would be a different story, a tougher assignment."

"Absolutely not," I assured him. "I just want to get people started on processes of necessary change. To bring the place a little closer to its peer colleges—a little closer to where most people think it is already.

"I can't predict what the response is going to be to the terminations," I said. "I think most faculty will be relieved and optimistic. Some faculty, the ones that benefited from the old system—the systemless system, really—may give you a very hard time. Do you have a thick skin?"

"Skins are thick in the SUNY system," he replied. "No problem."

"I assume you've worked in a multiracial environment," I continued. I wanted academic affairs and student services to work very closely together.

"Of course. Many of them."

"I can't predict what's going to happen with regard to the racial tensions. They're not going to go away. They could get worse as spring comes." I hadn't admitted that, even to myself, before now. I had once thought that all we needed to do was repaint the Founder's Plaque and replace a tired president, and tensions would evaporate.

I didn't think that anymore. Middleton College stood on its hill, high above the white communities that surrounded it: Fremont with its KKK heritage; Jefferson Mills, resolutely white and pursuing its policy of safe growth; the town of Middleton, where pedestrians stared at a black woman driving a big car, and whose police department insulted an administrative official of the college by keeping him waiting all night on a bench in the station.

Although it sat on a hilltop, Middleton College was not truly apart from the community, the way my old liberal-arts college was from its surrounding conservative community. Middleton College drew many of its students from just those towns and villages. Their parents were probably something like mine—decent hardworking people until the subject of race was raised. Then the stereotypes of a hundred years rose to the surface.

"I hope you'll come anyway," I concluded my conversation with Greg. "This is a defining moment for Middleton College. You can make a significant difference if you do." "Defining moment," "significant difference"—clichés of presidential rhetoric. This time they were true.

"I'd like to come," Greg finally said.

~

That Friday, the last day of final examinations, after most of the students had left, I called Bonnie and Harlan to my office individually, told them my decision, and asked Rhoda to send a press release to her usual list of media outlets right after I had distributed a memorandum to the faculty and staff. In the memo I said I'd have a general meeting of faculty and staff that afternoon to announce the names of the interim deans of academic affairs and student services.

CHAPTER 7

January: New Year, New Faces

Perhaps I should just have sent out the memorandum. What was the point of having a meeting? I couldn't tell the faculty and staff what had gone into the board's thinking and mine, in making these decisions. It wouldn't be fair to the college or to the people I had dismissed or to Phil Harkness.

Well, what I could do was to announce that two senior administrators of the college were being replaced. There was no ambiguity: they were gone; their successors had been named that very morning. That ought to be worth something in the candor department. Not much, maybe, but my memo and announcement were in clear contrast to the way such matters had been handled in the past: terminated employees just disappeared from the campus, and no one but the president was sure whether or not they'd be back.

The Founder's Room was jammed with people. The crowd wasn't identifiably hostile or friendly. Just noisy. I read a brief statement that included short bios of both Bryant Dunbar, whom they knew, and Greg Davidson, whom they didn't. Then I opened the floor to questions.

"Have Bonnie and Harlan been banned?" Jane Proctor asked.

"No," I replied.

"Are you going to get rid of other people too?" Ginny Jones asked. I winced at the phrase "get rid of."

"I don't intend to replace others," I said.

"You told us you were going to be open and aboveboard with us"—I could hardly see the questioner, but I think it was Martin Cobb from political science—"and then you hit us with this." The question seemed whiny. I adjourned the meeting after a few more questions. I thanked the group for coming.

The television crew from Echo River was waiting outside the door. Darlene Dawson was holding the microphone. She was a very attractive young woman and perhaps a talented one. After she had gathered me into her orbit, and the camera lights came on, she cast her face into an expression of utter sorrow.

"Why now? Only one week before Christmas. How could you do it?"

Because I am a savage person. I hate the holidays and I like to do my cruelest acts at that time. I only wish that Harlan's wife were about to have a baby, and Bonnie had a dying husband. Then my acts would have their most powerful effect.

That's what I wanted to say. Wouldn't that have gotten the attention of every viewer in the Echo River media market: the paragraph played and replayed; psychologists invited to have a panel discussion on channel four to explain how Middleton College could have invited so deranged a person to serve as its head. The psychologists would have disagreed among themselves, of course, and that would have made for really good television. There could have been a call-in program, with viewers expressing their interpretation of the president's words.

What I really said was "I'm sorry; this is a personnel matter, and I can't discuss it further with you."

Channel four did play the story a bit breathlessly on the six o'clock news, but there wasn't much to be breathless about, except that these actions had been taken right before Christmas. Like most of the local media and the regional newspapers, Darlene announced the terminations and speculated on the reasons. "In the aftermath of last spring's racial turmoil, two more administrators were forced to resign today," or "It is widely supposed that yesterday's resignations were connected with the racial problems that Middleton College had last spring."

No, you guessed wrong, or at least mostly wrong. You were probably led astray by a red herring—the fact that one white person, Bonnie Truesdell, was replaced by one black person, Bryant Dunbar. Admittedly, though, without last spring's incident, there would have been little news value in two administrators' being replaced.

As for the Grinch-stealing-Christmas spin, I'd just have to swallow hard and hope my friends would still be my friends when this hazardous tour of duty was over.

~

I stayed in Jefferson Mills over Christmas and New Year's. I'd originally hoped to get away to my cabin in Wisconsin for a few cozy days of snow and silence, but that couldn't be. Too much to do. When I came into the office on the day after Christmas, Flora Billings, the head housekeeper, was already there.

Flora and her family lived on a pig farm near Fremont, but she had worked for Middleton College for years. She had powerful shoulders and arms, a prodigious capacity for work, and a strong sense of self-esteem.

"You can't use the office for two days," said Flora. "I'm shampooing the carpets. Always do it between Christmas and New Year's. Everybody knows that."

"I'm new," I explained.

"Doesn't matter. The carpet's wet. I'll do the corridor next. That'll be wet, too. You might just as well go back home." I sensed a power struggle developing here, and I chose not to go head-to-head with Flora.

"Thanks, Flora. I will. The carpet looks really nice where you've been over it."

"You bet it does."

"Happy New Year," I called in farewell.

"Won't be New Year for six more days."

Let Flora have the last word, I warned myself. Don't be patronizing. Don't chuckle indulgently or ask her why she is shampooing my rugs for the third time since August. Was she a mole? For whom? My paranoia was showing. Just leave. I did.

When the carpets were dry I came back, and I completed the work I needed to do before Greg Davidson and Bob Brown joined the college and before I went to Florida for the President's Institute of the Council of Independent Colleges (CIC).

I'd gone to the CIC meetings every year that I'd been a president. The first year, I expected to meet a lot of large egos bumping each other like big balloons in small rooms and narrow hallways. I couldn't have been more wrong. The college presidents whom I knew were hardworking and conscientious and smart. They were conservative to the extent that they must conserve and, if possible, improve their institutions. They represented places like Middleton College, teaching colleges with small endowments and shaky enrollments, and they spent many sleepless nights worrying about aging boilers, thin-skinned faculty, and underprepared students. They had few buffers between themselves and the problems of their colleges: no layers of bureaucracy, no specialized personnel to meet specialized needs. They were always vulnerable, and their jobs were almost always on the line, in these times of expanding needs and shrinking budgets.

These times? When was it otherwise? Maybe thirty years ago, when the baby boomers came to college, but not since then.

The CIC had warned us all for years that our enrollments were going to shrink until the turn of the century, and they were going to shrink beyond our colleges' capacity to survive if we didn't vigorously recruit the kinds of students most of us never had sought before—members of minority groups. Recruiting minorities was the right thing to do, but it was also a key to maintaining enrollment.

Many presidents had done just that. They had persuaded conservative Boards of Trustees that their little colleges had to embrace diversity. Sometimes they had to persuade themselves first. A few had silently resisted, because they knew that increasing the numbers of minority students almost invariably produced conflict of some kind. (On the other hand, conflict has always been part of college life. Simply gathering numbers of young people in one place almost assures some kind of clash, even if it's only against fuddy-duddy professors and rule-making administrators.) Could these college presidents be faulted if they approached diversity cautiously? They wouldn't be allowed too many mistakes, and they didn't have many experts they could consult if trouble came. Middleton College and its April Incident—nearly everyone here knew about it—must have seemed like the thing the diversifying presidents feared. There it was, the beast in the jungle that had come out and devoured a president.

At the closing banquet of the President's Institute, awards were given to the individuals and foundations that had done the most to advance the well-being of small colleges. This year, the highest award of the CIC went to Bill and Camille Cosby for the twenty-million-dollar gift they had made to Spelman College, an all-black women's college in Atlanta. Their goal, they said, was to encourage other wealthy African Americans to support higher education.

I sat at a table with presidents from two all-black colleges. (Actually, the higher-education community calls them historically black colleges and universities, HBCUs, because they cannot legally exclude whites.) Both men were near retirement, and both were reminiscing, especially about the days of the civil rights movement. Myer Titus, president of a small black Methodist college in Little Rock, had tutored the nine students who desegregated Central High School in 1957, to help them keep up with their white classmates. "I've stayed in touch with all of them," President Titus mused. "They're all good people and they'll go to heaven happy."

Here was the president of a segregated college who, thirty-five years before, had worked overtime to make integration succeed.

Was this a contradiction? I didn't think so. There's a place for both. Black colleges do for black students what women's colleges do for women. All the studies that have been done of the effects of women's colleges show that twice as high a proportion of women "achievers" attended women's colleges as attended coeducational institutions. Women's colleges have made much of this, as well they should, although the explanations they give are impressionistic and anecdotal, not as quantifiable as counting achievers, whom you can look for in places like a Who's Who.

Women's self-esteem is significantly enhanced by attendance at a women's college. Women are not inhibited from speaking up in class; women hold all positions of responsibility in student government and student organizations; they study with a faculty that is largely female; and their speakers at commencements and convocations usually are successful women.

Equally important, attendance at a women's college does not mean that the graduates stay in a sex-segregated world. Most of them marry, many attend coeducational graduate schools, and, in recent years, many have succeeded in fields once closed completely to women.

I extended the same reasoning to black colleges and universities. I'd talked to Bryant Dunbar about this issue, and he told me that the research literature supported my conclusion. Separate colleges, and separate organizations within colleges, tend to produce graduates with higher self-esteem, better able to make their way in a society in which they are still a minority.

My thoughts about this were no mere mental exercise.

Some of the African American students at Middleton College were petitioning for a separate Black House. The issue had already come before the student affairs committee of the Board of Trustees, and its chair, Ernie Newman, was opposed.

"Why don't more of you join the existing sororities and fraternities?" Ernie had asked during a committee meeting just before Christmas vacation. I had attended the meeting.

"We don't like the way they have parties," Don Thomas, spokesman for the African American students had explained. "We don't like parties that are just about drinking. We don't like their music and they don't like ours. We want to be with the brothers . . . and sisters." I thought about what Lucas Henderson had told me: at one time Donald had just about decided to join one of the mostly white fraternities.

The issue had been tabled, but it wasn't going away. Ernie and most of his colleagues on the board were dead set against anything that smacked of separatism. They believed that separatism would just "make matters worse," whatever that meant. I thought they were partly right, but I believed that separatism denied would be still worse, and I didn't believe it was an issue worth debating. Black Houses are common on many campuses. So are Jewish Houses and Latin American Houses. In my college days, and on the campuses where I taught, we often had a French House or a German House, and nobody ever complained that these were unduly divisive. Students who lived there were, college administrators assumed, improving their language and cultural skills.

~

The second semester began the day after I returned from the CIC meetings. The state legislature reconvened shortly afterward, and I had a call from Peter Higgins, the chief lobbyist for the private colleges and universities in the state.

"The legislative black caucus wants you to come and meet

with them about what you're doing to strengthen Middleton College. Are you willing?"

"Sure. At their convenience. Is there somebody I should call, or can you set it up?"

"I'll call Sam Powell," Peter replied. "He's the head of the caucus. He also controls the allocation of money under the Remedial Education Act. Middleton applied for some of that money a couple of years ago but didn't get it. I'll get back to you after I talk to Sam."

Before he did, I met Representative Powell in the state capital at the Martin Luther King Jr. birthday celebration, a huge luncheon to honor Dr. King and community black leaders. Middleton College had never been represented, but this year, at Rhoda Dillard's suggestion, we had bought a table and brought a group that included students and administrators.

Rhoda went off looking for Sam. He wasn't hard to find, because a television crew, lights blazing, was following him through the crowd. He made his way over to the Middleton College group and shook all hands. I took that as a good sign.

"I'm looking forward to meeting with the black caucus," I said, after we'd been introduced.

"Come to my office on the hill next week," he said, "and we can talk about that. Rhoda maybe can set that up. We're good friends—been on the same wavelength a long time. Her husband's in the State Department of Education. Known him even longer."

"Fine," I said. Rhoda nodded.

When the luncheon and the speeches were over, we sped back to Middleton because at last the Multicultural Center was about to open. Since August, it had been talked about, planned, promised.

Maybe the reason for the delay in setting up the center was that nobody knew just what it was supposed to be, or what it was supposed to do. In fact, as I thought about it, there had been delays in defining and keeping several of the promises that had been made the previous summer.

The diversity committee, for instance. I sat in on a couple of its meetings during the first semester. I wasn't sure how the ten members had been chosen, because the committee was up and running (well, up) when I arrived in August. Lucas Henderson from sociology chaired the committee, and one or two of the other members were also white. The rest were African American students and one or two other faculty members. They helped organize the sensitivity-training sessions that Bryant's wife, Betty, conducted in the residence units.

The meetings I attended, though, went no place. Worse than faculty meetings: What is diversity? What should diversity be at Middleton College? We don't want attention paid only to African Americans (Lucas speaking). General silence. No, diversity's gotta mean everybody, all kinds (Donald Thomas). More silence.

I decided that my presence floated the diversity snowflake onto a warm surface, so I quit coming.

The sensitivity training seemed stalled, too. In mid-December, a contract had finally been signed with Central State University's Office of Minority Research to evaluate the racial climate at Middleton and then to prescribe a course of action that its office would direct. CSU had put out a press release after the contract was signed, and the region's newspapers had carried articles with headlines like "Central State Will Assist Troubled Middleton Cure Racial Ills." I groaned. I groaned and called the president's office at CSU. The president was unavailable. Could his assistant help me?

"Any press releases regarding this contract must be jointly issued," I said. "We are your client, not the heathen dwelling in darkness. Would you communicate that to President Althaus?"

Yes, he would. The assistant didn't say he was sorry; no

people in positions of responsibility these days say they are sorry, lest they have admitted to something for which they may later face litigation.

The evaluation of "racial climate" began early in January, with telephone interviews of faculty members: interviews done by graduate students; stupid questions, thought the faculty, and designed so poorly that they would reveal nothing of value. The faculty hated them, and they let Bryant (whom they held responsible) know just how inept they thought the interviews were. Some of the complaints, voiced at the January faculty meeting, subtly hinted that someone with an Ed.D. (not a research degree, like the Ph.D.) would not be equipped to judge the merit of such research as the CSU Office of Minority Research was now carrying out.

But the Multicultural Center was going to open. For the time being, it was going to be a resource center, a place that students could go to talk and read about multicultural issues.

The center was in a former storage area on the north side of the dining hall, and it was about the size of a large classroom. With the money appropriated by the trustees the summer before, bookshelves and easy chairs, end tables and table lamps, some books and posters, had transformed the area into a warm and appealing gathering place. Considerable emphasis had been put on the "multi" of "multiculturalism." All minorities of color were represented in the posters and art objects. I'd contributed a few books, and I knew Rhoda had given some Kenyan carvings.

The place was jammed with people on opening day. A brief program had been planned. Greetings were brought from nearby colleges, and Evelyn Hart, the board chair, gave a welcome and congratulations to the people who had made the center possible. I said a few encouraging words and introduced Bob Brown, the new director of multicultural services. He said good things about multiculturalism. He'd be in charge of programming for the center. If you had ideas for programs, talk to him.

Then, unannounced, Donald Thomas came to the platform. He looked happier than I'd seen him on other public occasions. He smiled sweetly at Evelyn and me.

"I am here because I want to tell you that I am no longer Donald Thomas. I am Donald X. You are all probably wondering why I have done this, and what it means."

I felt a little uneasy.

"I have come to realize that Thomas is my slave name, and I reject my slave name. For now, my name will be X—symbolizing that which is unknown—and I will struggle to learn what my true identity is, and then I will choose the name that best fits my true identity." There was a smattering of applause, most of it from the African Americans in the audience, when Donald concluded his remarks and stepped down.

Rhoda, whose grandmother knew the Thomas family, had told me a little more about Donald than I had known before. His parents had died when he was very young, and he'd been raised by his grandmother and two aunts. Their lives were totally wrapped up in two things: Donald and an evangelical black church in Echo River. They were very proud of Donald, the first person in the family to attend college, but they weren't quite sure what he studied at Middleton. I wondered if they were aware of Donald's name change.

I walked back to my office with Evelyn Hart.

"Went pretty well," she said. A brief pause. Then, "Did you expect Donald to make his speech? That really surprised me."

"I didn't expect it," I said.

"Do you think it means anything more than just what he said?" she asked with just a hint of anxiety in her voice.

"I don't think so. He's a pretty extroverted kid, and he was testing his verbal muscle in front of a sympathetic audience. If anything, it's probably a good sign. He's maybe a role model for some of the African American students who still feel marginalized here, even with all our efforts to bring them into the mainstream. I think there's been some foot-dragging about keeping the promises that were made last summer. The zip has gone out of the people who were charged with the task of implementing them."

"Has anyone complained to you about that?" Evelyn asked.

"No," I replied. "But it could happen: one day somebody like Donald could get up in some meeting or other and complain that the college is showing bad faith. That might not be all bad—unless this hypothetical speech is covered by all the major networks."

"Changing the subject," Evelyn said, "have you and Lisa presented Lisa's report to the faculty yet? The one you and she told me about before Christmas?"

"Next week."

"Another change of subject: how does the second semester enrollment look?"

"Not too bad. We're down a little, but we have a number of transfer students. Sometimes the admissions counselors get carried away, though, in their recruiting. Would you like to hear a funny story about that?"

"A funny story would be welcome."

"One of the transfer students went to Columbia Community College. She loved the idea of coming to Middleton, and her parents were willing to pay the additional tuition so she could attend a private college, but she wanted to be sure she could pursue the major she'd decided on."

"Which was?"

"Music appreciation for the hearing impaired. Josh, the counselor who recruited her, assured her she could meet the requirements for that here, except for learning sign language. She'd have to take that at night at Columbia. So she's here.

Except her car has broken down. Josh is driving her to sign language class."

"I don't think that's terribly funny," said Evelyn, but she did smile. "Is there really such a major somewhere?"

"Apparently."

We chuckled and shook our heads in a kids-will-be-kids manner, and Evelyn left.

~

More serious student problems than this were all around me. Because my office was on the first floor of a multipurpose building, I probably heard and saw more students, and learned of more student problems, than if I had been in a separate administration building.

Every college and university has troubled students. Many come to college with sorrowful and intractable problems: drugs and alcohol, divorcing parents, suicide attempts, questions of sexual identity, and sometimes histories of sexual abuse. Some among their families and friends have AIDS or are HIV positive. Racial tension has given an extra twist to the stresses and disorder that haunt many of today's undergraduates.

Before Christmas, a young white woman said she was being stalked by the black freshman who had bothered Sally Murphy in class. For a few days she refused to use the showers on her floor, because she believed he was waiting for her there. Her RA, even though she was spooked herself by the allegations, went into the shower to see. Nobody there. All clear. But the story had spread, like a tipped paint pot, that a black man was stalking a white woman. Both the white woman and the black freshman dropped out of college at the end of the first semester.

Now, in the dark days of January, I began to hear of other problems. Thefts. Sweaters and jewelry were reported stolen, and the thief, another student, then wore them conspicuously around the campus, in front of their owner. When confronted by the RA, she said she'd been forced by the real thieves to wear the clothes. The real thieves, tall muscular men wearing ski masks, she said, had bound and gagged her and told her she must take the rap or they'd beat her up. This was about the worst alibi I'd ever heard. She returned the clothes, promised to seek psychological counseling, and the matter was dropped.

A few days later, more thefts were reported. This time a student's jewelry was taken, and she called the police when she saw the jewelry in another student's room. She was not about to forgive and forget. Bryant told me she was going to press charges, and the college would have to remove the thief from the residence hall. He had asked Chief Janowicz to help him evict her. I heard the chief clanking up the stairs on a Thursday afternoon, and a little while later, clanking down again.

"Where is she now?" I asked Bryant later. "Where's her home?"

"She doesn't have a home, really. She's in jail now. She confessed. Her parents are dead, and her brother's in prison."

Wasn't there something else we could have done? Counseling? Did she have any other living relatives? Who was paying her tuition? I never learned what became of her. After a few days I stopped thinking about her.

Rhoda's Kenyan carvings disappeared from the Multicultural Center about this time.

"Does Bob or Bryant have any idea who might have taken them?" I asked.

"No. They're not much interested." Her voice had an edge to it that I had not heard before.

"Let's do *something*," I insisted. "Put up notices, send out a memo, something."

"They're not interested in doing that. They've got more important things to do."

"You draft the memo, I'll send it out over my signature—something about a reward for information, or bring the carvings back no questions asked. You know."

Rhoda nodded.

I knew it was foolish for me, the president, to become involved in trying to solve petty thefts or arouse community interest in restoring stolen property. *I* had more important things to do. My platter was overflowing. A board meeting, a state-of-the-college address, a general meeting with the faculty to present the information that Morgan Enrollment Advisors had gathered, and then beginning the planning effort that Greg Davidson was going to direct.

I sent out the memo. If I didn't, it seemed no one would, and shouldn't something like this be announced to the whole campus? The carvings were never seen again, but security was increased around the Multicultural Center. It was only open a few hours a week, and student workers or Bob Brown or some other administrator had to be around when it was.

Take comfort, I told myself. Since the Security Incs. had been hired, the campus thefts of recent years had not recurred—the thefts of big stuff like computer equipment. I didn't take much comfort. The residence-hall thefts, the theft of the carvings, on the heels of everything else that had happened since the college year began, lent an air of uneasiness and misfortune to the campus.

I took some comfort from the way in which my new appointees were taking hold, especially the two I had known the least about. Brown was tireless, and the minority students seemed to like and trust him at once. In less than a month, he had set up a series of programs to take place in the Multicultural Center, and he had asked to give an all-college convocation to kick off Black History Month. He was on campus every day and well into the evenings. He had lunch and dinner with the minority students in the college dining hall on most weekdays, and wherever he went at Middleton College, he was accompanied by a group of admiring black men and two or three black women.

Davidson was also working hard. He read through all the files, met with the administrators who reported to him—the registrar, the director of remedial services, the head of the computer center—and met with each faculty member individually. They liked him. Even professors who had been particularly close to Greg's predecessor were civil and even helpful.

His relationship with Bryant was another matter. I had begun to worry about that. I had hoped that the two men would work well together—they had liked each other when they first met—particularly on a grant application for state remedial education funds. But when the deadline came, Greg got the proposal in, and told me vaguely that he'd finished it himself.

Now was the time to present the Morgan report to the faculty and staff. That would be the first step in bringing about the admissions and retention goals the consultants had set. Many of the procedures, requirements, courses, and services of the college needed to be redesigned, and they had to be redesigned through a campus-wide, consensus-building enterprise. Representatives from the faculty, staff, administrators, and alumni would form the planning team. Students would be welcome as observers and resource persons. The effort would be directed by Greg Davidson. Fred Farnsworth would provide the necessary data backup. Anybody could attend the meetings, and anybody could speak or raise questions when the main part of each meeting was over. Each meeting would last two hours and would be directed toward agreeing upon two or three recommendations to the president. If I accepted them, the recommendations would find a place in the next year's budget; if they were policy matters, I would bring them to the board.

"Let me show you what your problems are," said Lisa, and

began a four-hour presentation to the faculty and senior administrators, complete with slides and overheads, circles and arrows.

When it was over, she answered questions, and when the questions were over, Greg Davidson took over the meeting.

"This information will be available in the library," he said, "for those of you who want to look at it in a more leisurely way or for those who couldn't come today."

I wasn't at the meeting, so I had to rely on others to report on how this had all gone over. Lisa thought everyone was fascinated with the data. Greg thought people were energized by the report. Bill Solomon, who came by the next day, even though we weren't serving wassail any longer, thought it was the best four-hour meeting he'd ever attended.

CHAPTER 8

February and March: Other People's Agendas

The best hairdresser in the county was Arlene at the Mane Attraction in Fremont. Alice May Peterson, director of development, had told me that. Whenever I went there, which was every couple of weeks or so for a shampoo and styling, I felt as if I were entering a radio show of my childhood—*The Great Gildersleeve*, perhaps—or one of the small Iowa towns where my aunts and uncles and cousins lived. The Mane was a unisex shop (there was the flaw in my reminiscence: the term was unknown in those earlier days, and the concept was unthinkable), with two barber chairs for men, and two styling chairs for women. I was never disappointed with the work of my hair designer (another contemporary term), though the general appearance of the shop was not inspiring. Jimmy, the owner, swept the shop once or twice a day, and the accumulation of hair between sweepings was a daily record of the clientele.

I sometimes imagined Chief Janowicz of Middleton, on the trail of some malefactor, sorting through the debris of hair, finding exactly the swatch that matched the handful gripped in the clenched fist of the dead victim. Would such evidence be admissible in court, I wondered idly as I pursued my imaginings, or was it a violation of privacy? Would the chief need a search warrant? What made the Mane seem like the locale for a sitcom was the parade of regulars that entered the shop on a typical afternoon. First came the postman, dropping off the month's bills, bantering amiably with Jimmy about whether he'd be able to pay them. Next came the salesman for YoungBeauty products, flirting gently with Arlene as he urged her to buy a few trial bottles of Protein Repair for Damaged Hair. The man getting a haircut talked about the prospects for the deer season, and the woman having her hair frosted talked about how irritated she was when hunters crossed her posted property without permission, but what could a person do? Arlene's two grade-school children stopped by on their way home from school, and she gave them their marching orders: a grocery list, a reminder about undone chores and piano practice, and an inquiry about homework. Sometimes everyone in the shop joined in a lively discussion about the high school football team. Arlene's son Matthew was the quarterback of the Fremont Marlins. His photograph, of a fierce-looking sandy-haired boy in full football battle dress, was on the shelf in front of her mirror.

Could such a town really have a KKK chapter? Entertainment of the 1950s didn't present such unhealthy possibilities. I had been told, though, that a chapter had existed in Fremont since the 1920s, an era when many small midwestern towns formed Klans that were antiblack, anti-Catholic, and anti-Semitic. On the afternoon following the April Incident, a KKK car had parked at the curb outside of Cutter Hall. Now, in the warm tranquillity of the hair sprayer softly rinsing shampoo suds down the drain, I tried to remember how anyone knew the occupants were from the Klan; they weren't in pointy hats and sheets. I'd ask Fred Farnsworth. He's the one who'd told me about their visit.

I have never been a good conversationalist at beauty salons. Usually I close my eyes and let the talk go on around me, and that's what I did at the Mane. Early in February I had a perm, and in the two and a half hours required, I had time to reflect, behind my closed lids, on where we stood at midwinter.

February was Black History Month, and I was encouraged by the list of speakers and workshops that Bob Brown had already scheduled. I'd attended the first one, a lecture by a visiting scholar on Carter G. Woodson, the father of Black History Month and for three decades the editor of the *Journal of Negro History*, and I had been impressed with the attendance. Most of the African American students came, and they asked many questions, the kind they never would have asked of a white speaker or in a predominantly white audience, the kind of questions that revealed some of what was really in their hearts. Have black Americans really done significant things, or have some of these old historians just made up stuff to make black people feel better? If African Americans have, why haven't we learned about them before now?

Very few white students or faculty attended. Just yesterday I received a gratifying letter from the speaker: I was the first white college president, he said, who had ever attended one of his lectures. He congratulated me.

Brown was on the calendar to give a talk soon, on black studies and multiculturalism. Scheduled at the regular convocation hour, Bob's lecture wouldn't conflict with any classes or athletic practices, so maybe he would have a good turnout.

Other developments were more troubling. African American students had begun to report campus racial incidents to me every week. Why to me and not to the dean of students? I wondered. One student said she had come out to her car and found it had been spat on by white students. How did she know it had been spat on? The spit had frozen in place. How did she know white students had done it? I asked. Who else would do it? she replied. A few days later, she came back to my office: one of the tires on her car had been slashed. My secretary went out to look at the car and reported to me that the tire hadn't been slashed; it had a simple flat. She asked building and grounds to send someone to tow the car to the Mobil station, but the student drove off on the flat to the station. Then another student came to report that she had been carrying a bag of groceries from Dick's Supermarket up Main Street to the campus, when a pickup truck ran her off the road. She didn't have a chance to note the license number of the pickup, or even its make or color. She dropped out of school the next day. Her mother came to get her and her things. I talked to Bryant Dunbar about these matters at our next meeting. "Why did the student say her tire had been slashed? My secretary looked at it. It was only a flat."

"I looked at it, too," he answered. "It was slashed."

Either it was or it wasn't, but I hadn't seen the tire myself.

"And there is the other student who said she was run off the road, but she couldn't give any description of the pickup—color, make, license number, or state. We need to get to the bottom of these things."

"No point trying."

I was startled. "What?"

"No point trying."

"Why not?"

"It could be anybody. This place is so racist it could be anybody."

"You must hear things," I persisted. "The RAs must hear things, kids bragging about harassment. Who would be doing this?"

"It could be anybody."

"Then we need to generate some discussion about the incidents, about the racial climate. Another round of sensitivity training, maybe?" That was the best I could think of on the spot. Shouldn't he provide some ideas?

"Okay. I'll get Bob Brown to schedule something." I could tell by the hunch of his shoulders and the twist of his mouth, he thought the exercise would be futile. In my heart I thought so, too, but I couldn't imagine doing nothing. How could he? I was astonished. Who was this person? I wondered silently. What had happened since October to fill him with such despair? And anger. Because he was angry. Was he getting flak because he was now the interim dean of students? Were Bonnie's friends giving him trouble?

The next day I had a call from one of the African American trustees, Darius Hawthorne. An extremely able lawyer, he had already announced that he would run for Congress in the next election. He would campaign to oust a longtime ineffective incumbent, and I wanted Darius to win.

"I had a call from a parent who lives in my district," he began, "and she told me what happened—her daughter being run off the road. She wants to enroll as a second-year student at a community college, but she needs her transcript from Middleton so she can get credit for the courses she took there."

I knew this story from Art Dove. "She can't get her transcript because she has an unpaid room-and-board bill here," I explained.

"Please release the transcript," Hawthorne said. "I'm sure the college doesn't want another media blitz because of a black student who is transferring because she got run off the road in Middleton. That could happen. The media blitz, I mean. That could be pretty damaging to the college."

"I'll tell Mr. Dove to release the transcript," I said. "Thank you for calling."

I called Art: "Release the transcript. Write off her bill as a bad debt. I've had instructions from one of the trustees." My stomach churned.

"Righto. I'll see that the registrar puts it in the mail this afternoon." No questions asked.

Arlene interrupted my reverie. "Let's take a test curl," she said, lifting the dryer.

"A couple more minutes," she decided, contemplating the limp curl that she had unwound, "and then we'll neutralize you."

~

The following week, Bob Brown gave his convocation address. He had a good crowd. Almost all the faculty were there, and many students. The African American students sat in the first three rows. They looked a heckuva lot more attentive (I thought enviously) than they had last August, when I gave my "Back to the Future" speech, or last month when I gave my state-of-the-college address in full academic regalia.

Bob wore a long khaki tunic and khaki trousers, and he wore a kente cloth around his neck and an African hat.

What a speech! Full of savage fury, most of it directed at the faculty. They had robbed African American students of their true heritage. These same faculty had foisted lies upon black and white alike. They had made false claims about Western civilization and now clung tenaciously to their lies in order to maintain white supremacy. Historians had glossed over the slave trade in their teachings, ignoring the central role of white people in making profit from human cargo.

(Ever seeking a ray of hope in the midst of this dark diatribe, I thought, Well, at least he hasn't hit the anti-Semitic theme. He hasn't blamed the Jews for slavery.)

Now, he continued, in a tone of voice that was alternately furious and mocking, the time had come to insist upon the truth, and Black History Month was the time and place to begin. All civilization began in Africa, and African students must claim their heritage. They must insist that it be taught in the classroom.

The first three rows cheered. Nearly all the faculty and all the white students sat in sullen silence. When the convocation finally ended, Greg Davidson and Rhoda Dillard and I walked out together.

"This is really serious," said Rhoda. "I'm worried."

"About what?" I asked. "He was pretty insulting to the faculty, I agree, but it's refreshing to hear a real stem-winder about academic matters, about what should be taught in the classroom. This sort of stuff has been said for years at other colleges. Welcome to the real world, Middleton College."

"Maybe. I'm worried about his talk of 'African students.' He means the African American students here, at Middleton. That's real radical stuff, calling them Africans. Things could get ugly, especially if the students pick up on it."

"The faculty is going to be mad as hell," Greg added. "They'll say he's wrong and ignorant and disrespectful."

"They weren't exactly fans of his to begin with," I reminded him, "or of Dunbar before him. They poked and needled whenever they got the chance. Tried to discredit him, and what he was trying to do. Maybe they deserved a dose of their own medicine."

"Don't tell them that," Greg warned.

"I wouldn't dream of it!"

The results of Bob's talk, and his leadership as director of multicultural services, seemed entirely salutary to me. I first saw the results of his efforts in the strategic-planning group of the college. The ground rules, set by Greg in consultation with me and the other members of the cabinet, were simple:

The group, which we named the Action Team (corny, but we didn't want anyone to think this was going to be another talk fest only) consisted of the cabinet, an alumnus, an elected group of faculty, and three noncabinet-level administrators. It met each week for two hours. The meetings were open to anyone who cared to attend, but nonmembers could not contribute to the discussion or raise issues until they had sat through the initial two hours, or unless they were asked to contribute by the chair.

Greg moved the meetings slowly but deftly. The overall goal of the planning group was to recommend changes that would be necessary to meet the needs and expectations of the anticipated increase in enrollment for the coming fall. The meetings moved slowly, because the goal was to reach a consensus on recommendations that the group would make to me. I usually sat in on the discussions.

The week after Bob's convocation, a group of African American students began coming to the planning meetings. They sat quietly for the required two hours and then, each week, raised issues of their own. I marveled that they were present at all. Usually the black students at Middleton College were conspicuous by their absence from college events, except as football and basketball players and fans. Marginal. That's the word. They were at the margins of college life, whether by choice or necessity, and nobody missed them. Now, some of them were participating in one of the most important, but tedious, activities of the college: strategic planning. Planning for the future of the institution.

In the early weeks, a designated spokesman of the black students would ask: What do your decisions today have to do with improving the quality of life and education that African American students receive at this college? At first the Action Team fumbled and mumbled in reply. Then members of the team became more responsive and internalized the questions they knew would be asked. They still didn't do very well at answering them.

After a few weeks I began to hear that some white students thought that only black students were permitted to attend these sessions.

That, of course, was not true. Everyone on campus received a memorandum explaining the ground rules. Copies of the memo were on every bulletin board and in every issue of the college newspaper, the *Weekly Wildcat*.

The rumors persisted, but no white students came to test them to see if they were true. Week after week, the black students continued to attend. For two hours they sat quietly; then their challenge would begin: We want significant curricular change. We don't want just a mishmash of multiculturalism. We want our heritage. We want the faculty to start telling us the truth.

The faculty members on and off the committee did not seem nearly as pleased as I was over the fact that the minority students had found their voices.

Donald X had become the most zealous of all. His actions went far beyond the Action Team's meetings. The college's presidential search committee was bringing promising candidates to campus now. Part of their day on campus was luncheon in the college dining room with a group of students and faculty. When the hapless candidate, ever smiling, ever responsive, began his or her lunch, Donald X would stride over from the African table and shout, "What are you going to do about the curriculum?"

The first time this happened, the candidate was taken totally unawares. He didn't need to be a rocket scientist to know what Donald had in mind, but the surprise of it infuriated him.

"Young man," he said, "you are being insufferably rude."

"What are you going to do about the curriculum?"

"Curricular change takes time," the candidate replied. "The faculty and the chief academic officer craft the curriculum."

Wrong answer.

"We've waited three hundred years," Donald continued, uninterested in the niceties of academic governance.

The African table cheered.

The next candidates who came to campus were warned in advance by the search committee that this might happen, and indeed it did. With the element of shock and surprise gone, subsequent candidates could be statespersons. Sit down and let's talk further about this, said one. May I discuss these important matters with you and your classmates, said another. Then the chair of the search committee could say, "There isn't time now, but there will be an hour later this afternoon when we'll talk about your ideas for changes in academic programs. Donald, you're welcome to join us then." His rhetoric de-escalated at once.

Donald was scheduled to share the convocation platform with Joe Cabot early in March. Each was to talk about last summer's internship: Joe with the Fish and Wildlife Service in Alaska; Donald with Jesse Jackson in Washington, D.C.

Donald's grandmother and two aunts had driven over from Echo River to hear him speak. They sat in the second row of the auditorium, and they were dressed as if for church. A few white students nudged each other, and nodded their heads toward the three women. "Check that," I overheard.

Joe's talk was just what I expected. Excellent, well organized, accompanied by slides. Although he seemed a little shy when he began, he gained confidence as he went on. His voice grew stronger, more earnest. He was well spoken, and clearly interested in the Alaskan salmon fisheries and the environmental challenges they presented.

Donald X was a surprise. He gave a sermon. He dispatched his announced topic within thirty seconds: "I met Jesse and told him about Middleton College, and he said he'd heard about the racism here."

Then Donald told his own story anew, about why he had changed his name. Since January he had developed further. He had become a Black Muslim. For the next twenty minutes, without a note or a pause, Donald talked about his new faith and called others to it. He waved, he pointed, he begged, he threatened, like the preachers he'd heard since childhood. He was very good. Where Bob Brown had lectured in a cold, accusing rage, Donald preached. When he finished, he was cheered by the other black students and his aunts and grandmother, and met with scattered applause by everyone else. When the convocation ended, I went up to the front to introduce myself to Donald's family. We all shook hands. They glowed with approval. If they were troubled by his new name and new religion, they showed no signs of regret. He was their star and their pride.

Thirty minutes later, Joe Cabot and his best friend, Hank O'Rourke, came to my office.

"I made him come," said Hank. "He didn't want to, but I said, 'You've got to tell her. It just isn't fair.' "

Were those tears in Joe's eyes? He spoke accusingly to me: "You went up and shook hands with those people and praised Donald—I heard you—and he didn't even talk about his subject. I did, I did just what I was supposed to do. You didn't say a word to me."

How did I feel? I felt terrible. What did I say? "I'm truly sorry. I always try to meet parents and relatives when they're here, and that's why I went up and introduced myself. My greeting had nothing to do with anything but that. If your parents had been here I would have done the same. Your talk was excellent; well organized, and very clear, even to nonscientists like me. Really well put together. I hope you get a chance to give it again—to some high school science students perhaps, to encourage them to go on to college."

There was nothing more to say. All three of us got up from our chairs. All three of us shook hands, and they left. I looked out the office window, across the piles of dirty snow, across the lane that bordered the back of the campus and the college cemetery. I could see the gravestone of the founder, Phineas Lowell. He had died of malaria six months after he founded Middleton College.

"Well, Phineas," I murmured, "things are a lot more complicated than you ever thought they would be. I hope you're sleeping well."

My secretary knocked on the door frame of the open door and came in.

"When you start speaking to the dead, it's time for a drink," she said.

"Good idea. Something with quinine water. To prevent malaria."

~

By the end of February, the campus-racial-climate survey was completed, and the results were made public. Eighty-one percent of faculty and staff and seventy-five percent of students believed that race relations on campus had improved over the previous year.

Eighty-one percent of students and sixty-one percent of faculty and staff agreed that "People tend to make too much of racial tensions on campus." The percentage agreeing with the statement was less for the minority respondents (fifty-nine percent) than for the majority (seventy-nine percent).

What percentage of the faculty and staff had actually been surveyed? Well, that wasn't entirely clear. Whoever happened to be at home the night the interviewer called, it seemed. I was disappointed.

The diversity committee continued its desultory meetings, trying to decide what to do next. Betty Dunbar returned to campus to do sensitivity-training sessions at the Greek houses. From the fragmentary news that reached me from the students who stopped by to see me once in a while, the sessions did not produce a noticeable rise in sensitivity. Irritation maybe, but not sensitivity.

As Black History Month drew to a close, Women's History Month rose like a bright new constellation in the late-winter sky. Jill Henderson had helped some of the women students organize a chapter of the National Organization for Women (NOW), and they were preparing a series of events. The NOW chapter, I had learned, had no African American members. Their opening workshop, on women's studies and the curriculum, was planned for the first week in March.

Feminism was a frail flower at Middleton College, and few women students would apply the word to themselves lest it be somehow misunderstood. Cheerleaders and sorority sisters fared best in the prevailing air of male athleticism.

I knew a few of Jill Henderson's students better than a president can know most students. I'd lectured in her women's studies class a couple of times, on women's history once and on women's biography and autobiography another time. Two of the officers of the NOW chapter lived upstairs in the residential part of my building. Cindy Livermore, a freshman, was a devoted follower of Jill's. "She really opened my eyes so much," Cindy told me one day. "I never noticed things like sexism, I mean on this campus. I never really knew it was here. The sororities and fraternities are the worst. The women are just like, well like high school, giggling and flirting and all. They're not interested in our heritage, or how we're discriminated against or treated as sex objects. The fraternity guys like them that way."

When pledging began, Cindy came to tell me she had decided she wanted to belong to Zeta Pi.

"Really," I said. "I thought you were going to stay independent."

"I decided I could have more influence if I were inside the sorority system," she explained.

A few days later she was back to report on the rigors of pledge life. "The actives make so many demands that the pledges don't even have time to eat. We're getting faint from hunger. What can we do?"

"Why not tell them you need a few minutes to eat," I suggested.

"I'll try that," she said, and hurried away.

The president of the NOW chapter was made of sterner stuff. Angie Whiteside was a junior, majoring in political science, and she had never had any intention of joining a sorority. Angie came to me with a different problem.

"We want to hold our opening workshop for Women's History Month in the Multicultural Center. Mr. Brown and Dean Dunbar say we can't—it's for cultural events, and women's things aren't about culture."

"What?" I was thunderstruck at the arrogance. Were they trying to pick a fight? Of course they were trying to pick a fight. Perhaps we could regard the occasion as a teachable moment.

"Why don't you organize some kind of debate or discussion," I suggested, "about whether there is a women's culture. Feminist scholars have been theorizing about that for years. That could be a consciousness-raising event for all the women students here."

Dream on.

"Maybe so," Angie said in a discouraged tone of voice. Her doubt shone through even her effort to be polite. She really wanted me to call Dunbar or Brown or both and tell them to get down off their high horses and let the NOW chapter use the center.

I did call Bryant after she left. "Can this possibly be true?" I asked.

"I don't know," he said.

"Will you try to find out?"

"I think I remember now," he answered after a pause. "Bob Brown has scheduled the center for a meeting of the African Caucus at the time the NOW chapter wants it."

I was startled by the new title: from Black Caucus to African American Caucus to African Caucus in little more than a semester.

"So the women could have it if they rescheduled their workshop for another time?" I asked.

"I don't know."

"Will you please look into this?"

"Sure."

The NOW chapter didn't press its case, and neither did I. I couldn't be drawn into a conflict that would divide the campus further. The women held their workshop in the Founder's Room, which was scheduled by the president's office. They didn't have a debate about whether women had a culture or not.

~

Over in the office of the interim athletic director, Geri Schmidt was fighting another skirmish in the war between the sexes. When Ed Jason had been AD he had taken on some of the managerial responsibilities that were supposed to be done by Coach Lombardino in the off-season. (The off-season, in this case, lasted from November until April, from the end of football season until the beginning of baseball, which was the other sport that Lombardino coached.)

The rationale for excusing Lombardino from those menial tasks—arranging for referees, unlocking and locking up the athletic facilities as their use required, making sure that necessary equipment was available—was that he spent the winter recruiting football players to Middleton College. Now he seemed to have lost interest in recruiting, but he wasn't wild about the idea of doing the housekeeping tasks that Ed Jason used to do for him.

His job description was clear, however, and Geri Schmidt, who was teaching and coaching in addition to serving as AD, wanted him to do what he was getting paid to do.

"Little kids are getting into the gym and fooling around with the equipment," Geri said when she talked to me about the problem. "There's nobody there; nothing's locked up. I'm afraid we're going to lose equipment. I'm afraid some kids are going to get hurt. I've talked to Bryant about this. He's too busy or something. If you want to know, I don't think he's being very helpful. Any ideas?"

"Have you talked to Lombardino?"

"Sure. He says he's doing his job."

"But he's not."

"That's right; he's not."

"I guess you'll have to tell him you're keeping a record of his nonperformance of duties and that his performance review will be affected. I imagine the whole idea of a performance review will be a new concept. Do you have any misgivings about doing that?"

"Not at all."

"Thank you. Let's talk about this again in a couple of weeks—or sooner if you think it would be helpful."

In four more days I was going on vacation. I was going to California to visit my daughter. I was going to watch her run in the Los Angeles Marathon. Then I was going to rent a car and drive to the Anza-Borrego Desert and Sequoia National Park and Yosemite with my good friend Bob who was going to vacation with me. The weather would be sunny and warm in L.A. We might stop at Disneyland for a few laughs.

CHAPTER 9

April: The Cruelest Month

The Los Angeles Marathon in 1993 turned out to be an occasion of immense multicultural bonhomie. Bob and I had arrived the night before, and the next morning we drove with Betsy to South-Central L.A., where the race began. As start time neared, huge crowds of every hue swirled outside the starting area under a cloudless sky.

I said good-bye to Betsy, giving her hugs and kisses for luck, as she entered the chute that read "Runners Only" and headed for the starting line with thousands of others. The festivity and gaiety of the morning reminded me of a line from a favorite book of my childhood, one that I had read to Betsy too, *Ferdinand the Bull*: "Bands were playing, flags were flying, and all the lovely ladies had flowers in their hair."

Indeed it was so, here in South-Central, a year after the terrible riots that followed the jury's verdict in the Rodney King case.

Betsy had been living in West Hollywood then. The commercial street nearest her apartment had been a thoroughfare for the rioting crowds, and when I could finally get through to her on the telephone, I could hear the *pop-pop* of gunfire in the background. Two days after the disorders began, the National Guard was called out and guardsmen were stationed on the corner of every street where there were shops and restaurants.

"It seemed so weird," she had told me, "to have soldiers in riot gear, with rifles and bayonets, right on the corner of Pico and Fairfax, by my grocery store. Tears came to my eyes when I saw them; isn't that strange?"

A spirit of festival had almost overcome those memories, at least for today. Plenty of police were around, carrying their thirty-inch billy clubs. You could deliver punishing blows with those long clubs, without getting close enough for a trouble-maker to grab or stab you. That day the cops held the clubs horizontally, one hand at each end, to keep crowds from surging onto the streets of the marathon's route.

The marathon, a distance of twenty-six miles and three hundred and eighty-five yards, is a formidable test of discipline, training, and will. I had run seven of them, quitting after I had qualified for and run the Boston Marathon when I was fifty-one.

You might think that watching a marathon is about as exciting as watching grass grow, but that isn't so. There is high drama in every mile, even the first. Five minutes before the runners begin, the starting gun goes off for the wheelers—the disabled, paraplegic, and amputees in sleek racing chairs. Most of them are belted into their chairs, at the waist and around their legs, if they have legs. They wear leather gloves to spare their hands, which turn the wheels. These marathoners have large, well-muscled arms and shoulders, in contrast to the thin, wiry bodies of the runners.

Most of the wheelers are male, and most of them that I have seen are under forty years old. Above the waist, they look as tanned and fit as any athlete. It takes courage, as well as training and will, to be a wheelchair racer. The year that I ran Boston, the first two wheelers had somehow tangled their chairs when they came around the first curve of the race and fallen, and nearly all the others crashed and tumbled into them to make a pileup of steel, spinning wheels, and helpless men.

No one was seriously hurt, and nearly all of them reentered the race once they were straightened up and pointed on their way to downtown Boston.

Now, I watched the L.A. wheelers fly by, down the straightaway of Figueroa, seeking the inside curb, like racehorses pressing toward the rail.

The second starting gun is for the runners, and in the first row are the runners who are the fastest, the contenders. In recent years, African runners have dominated marathon running: short, incredibly wiry Ethiopians and Kenyans have won the big races, and they were out in the lead today. The winner would probably have to maintain a pace of fewer than five minutes a mile for more than twenty-six miles.

Then come the thousands and thousands of runners who are competing only with themselves. I couldn't even see Betsy go by. She was somewhere in those thousands.

Bob and I went to a Japanese fast-food restaurant to grab a bite to eat before heading to the finish line, a few blocks from the start. We were the only people in the restaurant, except for a black family eating noodles with chopsticks.

The weather was lovely and warm, too warm for running fast or comfortably for so long a distance. The times would be slow today.

People were already crowding along the fence of the homestretch when Bob and I arrived, about two hours into the race. We wanted to see the winners in every age group, as well as the overall winners, man and woman. A large Latino family was grouped ahead of us, calling encouragement and approval to Latino runners, some of whom wore the name of their country of origin on their singlet.

Father would clap and shout, "El Salvador," and the whole family would cheer. "Guatemala!" and another family cheer.

"Mexico!" More cheers.

Down the homestretch came a young woman. Father

turned around to me, clapped, and said, "Woman!" and we all cheered.

The whole afternoon was like that. The good humor of the spectators was as warming to me as the sun.

The temperature was ninety degrees by early afternoon. Betsy's time was slower than she had hoped, because of the unusual heat, but she was running well and looked strong as she came into view at last. She smiled and waved as she went past us, and we joined her in the happy mob around the refreshment tables.

The rest of my vacation was as pleasant and restorative as its beginning. Only in the Anza-Borrego Desert did we have an anxious moment, and that one was funny. Crossing the desert, we had stopped at Borrego Springs to get a six-pack of beer. We began to consume the beer while motoring on, contrary to all the laws of the land. Suddenly, in my rearview mirror, I saw a state police car, with lights flashing, motioning me to pull over. Like a couple of teenagers out joyriding, we did our best to hide the beer.

The cop issued a speeding ticket—we were going fifty-eight miles per hour in a fifty-five-mile zone. Bob or I might have argued, if we hadn't felt guilty about our concealed substance. The fragrance of beer suffused our little car, and both of us were mute. Actually we tried not to breathe. After the ticket had been written, and we had been cautioned about excessive speed, we were allowed to continue.

After we finished laughing, I looked at the ticket. Fifty dollars.

"That's harassment!" I cried.

"Lighten up," said Bob, still grinning.

"If we were black we'd be on our way to jail," I insisted, irrelevantly.

"If we were eighteen we'd be on our way to jail," Bob observed.

"So?"

"Circumstances alter cases."

"That's not the way the justice system is supposed to work."

"But that's how it does work."

We both tired of the argument within another minute or two. We stopped for gas at a ramshackle station that looked as if it had been the model for countless "Last Chance for One Hundred Miles" cartoons. We changed drivers, and when we went on, heading north to Sequoia, I read aloud from a paperback of John Muir's *Mountains of California.* "When California was wild," he wrote, "it was one sweet bee-garden throughout its entire length, north and south, and all the way across from the snowy Sierra to the ocean."

~

One of Middleton College's presidential candidates had come for a campus visit while I was on vacation, and another was scheduled the week after I returned. I had a long talk with each one, by telephone for the one I hadn't met, and answered any questions they had.

The Board of Trustees was scheduled to announce its decision on the April day that was the anniversary of the incident.

The African Caucus had plans of its own for that day. Bryant told me they were bringing in a "fiery speaker" (his term) from St. Louis.

"I wanted you to know," he said, "so you're not surprised. All the media will be here, I suppose, because it's the anniversary. He's a black nationalist."

"I appreciate being told. I don't have a problem with that," I said, "but I don't want any anti-Semitic stuff."

"No problem. There won't be." And there wasn't.

I have thought often of the ease with which I addressed the matter and the ease with which Bryant responded. A year later it might have been harder for Bryant to give me the assurances he did.

But this was 1993, and Middleton College. The fiery speaker did indeed arrive and delivered a separatist message. For the first half hour of the speech, white people were excluded. When they were then invited in, they found that the speaker was flanked by two Middleton students, African American. One stood on either side of the speaker, arms folded, scowls on their faces. Another out-of-town guest walked up and down the aisles of the auditorium brandishing a baseball bat, stopping in front of groups of whites and giving them a particularly dark grimace and an occasional audible snarl. Many members of the audience looked him up and down and chuckled, as though they were watching a show. I wondered if they would have chuckled over the brandishing of fraternity paddles.

I heaved an immense sigh of relief at the end of that day and the night—it was a Friday—that followed. Television and newspaper reporters and cameras had combed the campus looking for stories. They had hoped to cover the announcement of a new president, but the announcement couldn't be made until the candidate accepted the position and agreed to terms of a contract. That could take several days, and did.

The fiery speaker didn't appear on the television news because he'd excluded whites for the first part of his address, and all the cameramen were white. By the time the baseball bat was brought out, the media had given up waiting to be allowed in. They missed what would have been the most arresting visual of the six o'clock news. Instead, they turned their attention to me.

"What do you think the racial climate is like on this campus now, one year after the riot?" I was asked.

"Do black students feel safe now? Are they all likely to leave like they did last spring?"

Don't try to correct the misinformation; don't quarrel with

terminology or numbers. Corrections always come out sounding defensive. Being defensive can be made to sound worse than lying. Give reporters something easy they can print or tape.

"According to a scientific survey done by the Institute for Race Relations at Central State University, eighty-one percent of faculty and staff, and seventy-five percent of students believe that the racial climate is better now than it was a year ago." Scientific survey. It was about as scientific as a papal bull, but it was enough. Even if they talked to others who said the racial climate was disastrous, the survey might prevail as higher truth. In any case, they couldn't accuse me of evasion.

"Who's the next president going to be?"

Strom Thurmond, I imagined myself saying, just to liven up the interview. Don't be funny, the wiser part of my nature insisted. They'll tear you apart in print, saying that you made a joke out of the most vital issue of our day. They'll publish photos that make you look like one of the witches in *Macbeth*. They'll run videotape of you tugging at twisted pantyhose.

"The board chair will be announcing that in a day or two." I smiled, and so the first anniversary came and went without serious trouble.

We had missed an opportunity, I thought sadly when I was by myself again, driving home to Jefferson Mills. Could we have had some unifying activity on campus instead of the separatist speaker and his friend with the baseball bat? Who could have organized such an occasion? I realized that I still yearned for unity, even as I defended separatism.

It seemed obvious to me that clouds between black and white were gathering. The lightning rod that attracted the most electricity was Donald X, who, in addition to his other activities, was an RA in Cutter Hall. Rumor had it that he was meting out justice in ways that the white students considered discriminatory. The incidents themselves were trivial, compared to what had gone on during the first semester: a white student was banned from campus (bannings again, I groaned) for three days because he had brought the family dog to his room while his parents were on vacation. Bryant Dunbar had suggested the banning, I learned, and refused to meet with the boy's parents. No, not exactly. He agreed to meet with them but didn't keep the appointment. They were furious—they had driven ninety miles to see him.

A group of white RAs came to see me about the double standard they thought was being enforced among the residence-hall staff. They were earnest and respectful. Donald, they claimed, did not show up for meetings, he wasn't on duty when he was supposed to be, and Dr. Dunbar wouldn't do anything about it. It wasn't fair.

"We're not racists," they insisted.

"Let me look into what you've told me." By now I knew that separating truth from fiction would be no small task. There probably would be no documentation.

Parents called to express their indignation at what their white sons and daughters had reported to them. White alumni called to announce that they were cutting off the college without a penny if the stories they heard were true: Would I please find out if they were true? They may have been true, but they well may not have been true. A black alumnus called to tell me that he saw a black lawn jockey on the rooftop of his old fraternity house. I asked the fraternity president to please see that the offending figure was taken down. "We didn't know it was a symbol of slavery," he said. A week later, it reappeared, painted half white. "We did it to symbolize multiculturalism," he explained. "Take it down," I said.

~

One morning in April, I received a call from a parent that signified the beginning of a new level of anger and provocation. It came at 9:00 a.m., two weeks after the anniversary, one week after the chosen candidate had accepted the presidency of Middleton College. The caller was the mother of a black student. "My daughter reported to me what happened last night," she began, "and I want to know what you are going to do about it. Today. What steps are you going to take today?"

"I'm sorry. I don't know what you're referring to," I said quietly.

"Some kind of president you are. You don't even know what's going on at your racist college. Or else you're just lying. I'm going to call you back this afternoon, and by then you better be ready to tell me what steps you're going to take." She hung up.

I tried to reach Bryant, but he wasn't in his office. I called Rhoda, because there were already several messages from reporters this morning.

"What happened?" I asked her.

"I'm trying to find out," she said. "Some students called the media and told them there'd been a fight here, between blacks and whites at an intramural basketball game. That's all I know so far. I'll try to find out some more, so we can put out a press release. I'll get back to you as soon as I know something."

I took a call from another angry parent, and then one from a reporter for one of the metropolitan dailies: "I understand that black students are going to take over a building tomorrow to protest the firing of the director of multicultural services and present their list of demands. They're calling a press conference in the Multicultural Center."

"The director has not been fired," I replied, "and I have no intention of firing him. That wouldn't be my call anyway—Bryant Dunbar is his immediate boss, and he hasn't indicated any such intention to me. Perhaps you should talk to him first."

"The students said they had received death threats."

"From whom? If so, that hasn't been reported to me or any other official at the college."

"Are you saying you don't believe that death threats have been received?"

"No, I'm saying that this is the first I've heard of such threats." A dangerous response. Given a certain spin, the statement could come out sounding as if the casual reporter had found out critical information that even the president didn't know.

By lunchtime Rhoda and I had pieced together the bare bones of a story. Something had happened at a basketball game. Apparently Bryant had been at the game. That should make the job of finding out easier. We both sat down with Bryant in the dining hall.

"What happened last night over in the gym?"

"Racism happened, that's what happened." He looked grim and haggard.

"We need to know more than that," said Rhoda gently. "Did people get upset? What did they get upset about?"

"The white spectators questioned a referee's call. The ref was African American. They hooted and hollered. One of the white kids came out of the stands, onto the floor, and got in his face. The ref pushed him away. Lots of people poured out of the stands then." Bryant stopped. He poked his fork at his food and shook his head silently.

"What happened next?" Rhoda persisted. "We have to know."

"What's the point? It's racism. What more do you need to know?"

I left the table because I was angry and puzzled. There was a surreal quality to this. Perhaps he would speak more freely in front of Rhoda alone.

By the end of the day I had a more complete account of the incident. What happened next was this: After the spectators came onto the court, the blacks and whites didn't go after each other. They pulled the referee and the pugnacious fan apart. The scorekeeper ended the game then and there, and everybody went home. Not a punch was thrown. Nevertheless, the next morning a newspaper from a distant corner of the state printed a brief article headlined "Violence Flares Again at Middleton College."

A press conference had been scheduled, at noon on Friday, by the African Caucus. Donald X and Holly Washington were seated in front of microphones at a table at one end of the large room. Behind them a dozen black students were seated in rows, looking grim and determined. One held a photograph of Malcolm X; another held a copy of Andrew Hacker's book *Two Nations: Black and White, Separate, Hostile, Unequal.* In front of Donald and Holly, half-a-dozen television cameras stood ready to roll, and behind the reporters and cameras and technicians were all the Middleton College students, faculty, and staff that could be crowded into the Multicultural Center. Donald offered me a chair up front, just to the left of the cameras, but I declined and stood instead at the rear, surrounded by people taller than I, where I could less easily be observed or photographed.

Donald began cheerfully, "You from the media all came because you thought we were going to take over a building, but we're not, and it looks like Bob Brown isn't going to be fired either. But anyway the African students at Middleton College have a set of demands, because of what life is like for us here.

"Here's what we want: we want our safety to be guaranteed; we want more curricular change; we want judicial processes and resident advisors' systems improved to assure fair, just, and equal treatment; we want the conditions of racism to be removed. The things the college has done since last spring, which they never would have done if we hadn't forced them to, they're only window dressing."

He was just getting started! His mood and manner changed dramatically. "Once again the African students have had to take action on behalf of the entire college." What did that mean? He was doing this for everybody? "Independent consultants have shown that this college is unworthy to be accredited because the faculty is incompetent; they don't know anything about the courses they're teaching because they haven't even been educated to teach those courses. The new president who's just been chosen is incompetent, too.

"For this reason, the African Caucus has secured legal counsel and is suing Middleton College for miseducation."

Good grief. Donald had apparently gotten hold of the Morgan report, easy enough to do. It was available in the library for anyone who wanted to wade through it. I didn't know why he'd added the touch about the new president.

Then came the clincher: "If violence is necessary for us to achieve our goals, then we will resort to violence." A murmur of alarm swept the room. People looked at one another. The dozen African American students behind Donald and Holly stared out at the audience in attitudes of determination.

Donald finished his statement and indicated his willingness to take questions.

"How do you feel about the present administration at the college?" he was asked.

"We are quite satisfied. We can work with Gretchen."

I winced.

"Then where is the racist opposition coming from?"

"From the faculty, which is incompetent, and from the white students."

By midafternoon, four white students had called to tell me that they heard there would be some kind of violent confrontation in Cutter Hall that night. "I heard two black girls at lunch," said one young man. "I don't know their names but one of them is really heavy. They were saying, really loud, that they were sick of looking at white people. They wanted to get a gun and blow us away. That's what they said. I'm having a very hard time studying. If they don't like it here, I say let them go someplace else to college, some black college where they don't have to see white people." Donald and Holly called to tell me that there were death threats on their answering machines after they returned from the press conference.

Many students went home for the weekend after the press conference was over, a few more than usual perhaps. I asked Bryant to stay in town at the bed-and-breakfast, in case of trouble. He agreed, but he didn't like it. I didn't like it that he didn't like it.

I decided to come back after dinner and work in my office. Several African American students had urged me to authorize arming the Security Incs.; I had refused without a moment's hesitation. I asked Art to put on a couple more security guards for Friday and Saturday night.

"When is the latest that students are likely to come back to their dorm for the night?" I asked Ginny, the assistant dean of students.

"The bars all close at two a.m., and most kids are back by two-thirty or three."

"If there's going to be trouble, isn't it likely that it will happen then?"

"Probably. Some of them get pretty roaring, you know, and nearly all the white kids that live around here come from homes where there are guns. They hunt."

I was startled. "Have you heard anyone say they were going to bring guns on campus?"

"No," she said lamely. "I just meant it was a possibility."

I napped for a while in my office and then, around midnight, walked across the campus to Cutter Hall. The night was crisp and clear, moonless, so the stars stood out brightly. Maybe that's one definition of a small town—a place where there's so little light clutter that you can see the stars from Main Street. One of the security guards emerged from the shadows, whistling so he wouldn't startle me, and offered to escort me to the dorm.

A couple of RAs were in the lounge, just inside the front door, when I arrived. The decor of the lounge was Middleton minimal. Three or four soda and snack machines were on the far wall, and three or four vinyl couches with thin wooden arms were pushed up against the side walls. A Ping-Pong table was in the middle of the room. It reminded me of the lounge in the minimum-security prison I had once visited.

The RAs were surprised. "I just came over to see how you were getting along. How's the evening gone?"

"Pretty quiet so far."

"Let's play Ping-Pong," I suggested, and so we did, for about two hours, under the harsh fluorescent lights. The RAs played first, one at a time, and then a couple of students who had come in to watch. I lost every game, but every one was close. The group that gathered was good spirited, and I was having more fun than I'd had all day.

Around 2:00 a.m., a few kids came in, noisily, cursing amiably to one another until they saw me, after which they quieted down, hung around the Ping-Pong table for a while, and then went off down the hall.

I had become the reincarnation of those doughty housemothers of yesteryear.

Nothing even remotely frightening occurred in Cutter Hall that night, and at 2:30 I went home.

~

The morning papers were full of Donald and Holly's press conference, just as the television news had been the night before. Headlines: "Middleton College Faculty Called Incompetent" and "Middleton College Will Lose Accreditation Because of Incompetent Faculty" and "Consultants Affirm Middleton College Must Close."

The first paragraph of each story made it clear that some students had made these allegations, but the headlines themselves were inflammatory, and the allegations were repeated in great detail. The trustees must be furious. The faculty must be ready to skewer Donald and Holly.

I called Rhoda as soon as my head cleared and my anger subsided. "What's your recommendation? I can't let this go unanswered."

"No," she said, "you'll have to have a press conference. You'll have to defend the faculty, and the college."

I called Greg Davidson next. "What do you hear?" I asked.

"OOOOh are they mad. The faculty."

I resented the fact that Donald X had backed the college, and me, into a corner: his actions compelled me to make a statement of some kind. Worse yet, I resented the fact that Lisa Dunn's report on changes needed at Middleton College, which we had so confidently placed in the library for everyone to read as they wished, had now been twisted into a weapon to discredit the institution.

My press conference on Monday afternoon in the Founder's Room was as jammed as Donald and Holly's on Friday. Cameras galore. Pencils poised. Many students, black and white, many faculty members, looking grim, were awaiting my words.

I sat at a long table, with members of my cabinet beside me. Bryant was immediately to my right, and he looked miserable. He did not want to be here, up on this platform, sitting where he was sitting. You are the dean of students, I thought sternly, and this is where you're being paid to be.

I read a statement that described the basketball incident that had touched off the events of the last few days, and the claims that violence had been threatened. "During this academic year, there has not been a single fight or alleged fight, a single assault or alleged assault, in the residence halls or on this campus."

I addressed the demands that Donald and Holly had made. "Students had not previously presented these concerns to the administration, though several of the issues were already being worked on in the student services area, under Dr. Bryant Dunbar's direction, and in campus-wide committees."

Then I reached the heart of the matter.

"In the course of last Friday's press conference, the spokesperson for the African American students said that most of the faculty was incompetent, and that 'independent consultants' had declared the college unworthy of accreditation. He also declared that the newly selected president was incompetent." Pause. I directed my most withering gaze along the row of reporters. "Not a shred of evidence was presented in support of these reckless charges, nor did you ask for any.

"These charges and their appearance in print and sound bite are outrageous. This is the same faculty that was commended by African American students last spring for their assistance in helping them complete their semester's work in the aftermath of April's disturbances.

"In my presidency at Middleton College, I have come to know and admire many faculty members for their intelligence, hard work, and dedication to the college and its students. There is wisdom and foolishness in this faculty in about the same proportion as it exists in faculties at other colleges—and in the human race.

"We have accomplished a great deal at Middleton College this year. Some have called our efforts to make this a more truly multicultural environment only 'window dressing.' I'm here to tell you it is not window dressing. It is a foundation."

Cheers and applause. I recognized some of the RAs who had come to see me earlier, and some of the students who'd hung around the Ping-Pong table. Cindy Livermore and Angie

Whiteside were present, too, cheering and applauding. But the shouts of approval followed the color line. The black students were silent and sullen, and when the conference broke up, Donald and Holly strode out of the meeting, furious. The cameras followed, of course, and five minutes later, the two students were conducting a press conference of their own.

CHAPTER 10

May: Distress Calls

The next round of newspaper articles and television reports were far more measured and prudent than what had gone before. My remarks were repeated in some detail, and without any deprecating adjectives. The more strident claims of Donald and Holly (Rhoda had listened to them) did not appear in print. They continued to say that they had filed a lawsuit, and the media continued to report that they had, but not one was able to find out in what court it had been entered, or when it might be heard.

A reporter asked them whether they had discussed their concerns with the president. No, they said, she was a liar and a racist, and her word meant nothing. No point in discussing anything with her. Friday I was someone who could be worked with. Monday I was a scoundrel and a betrayer. That hurt.

Bob Brown had also become an object of public interest and attention, ever since his convocation address. While I was rejoicing in his ability to win the interest and attention of the African American students, Rhoda Dillard's antennae had told her he could become dangerously disruptive. He was working hard to awaken the African American students, and he was succeeding with some: they had become Africans, inheritors of all culture and civilization, deprived of their heritage, convinced that their college deserved to close if it would not meet their legitimate demands.

He didn't intend to hide his light under a bushel either. He had given a couple of interviews to newspapers.

The faculty's wrath grew to boiling when a new tactic emerged. The confrontations that had begun on the convocation platform and then had moved to the basketball floor now moved to the classroom. At the request of some of the African American students, who thought they were not being taught the truth, Bob began to visit some classes and then to send reports of the faculty's incompetence and racism he had observed to Greg Davidson, the chief academic officer. A typical allegation noted that a professor had told a member of the African Caucus who was failing his course, "You need to spend less time on your cause, and more time on this course if you expect to pass." Bob asked that these reports be made a part of the faculty member's permanent file.

Bob was most critical of the part-time African American professor who came to campus once a week from the state university to teach African American history. Bob fired off a memo—called a racial incident report—to Davidson after each meeting. Here, disagreement became allegation of incompetence. A sample: "America in the twentieth century has done more than any other nation to address its racial problems and seek justice and equality."

The real problem, I decided, after reading several of these incident reports, and sending memos to the faculty to assure them that Bob's reports weren't going in anyone's record, was that Professor Mallory was not a black nationalist. In my college days, during the prime of the House Un-American Activities Committee and then of Senator Joseph McCarthy, college and university professors had been dishonored and driven from their posts when they weren't "American" enough. Twenty years later, some professors were harassed if they were *too* American—too supportive of American policy in Vietnam and of the decision-making establishment.

Brown's visits and memos were pale stuff compared to

those other times of trouble. No fights, no boycotts, no marches. I couldn't tell whether or not he represented most of the black students, or only a few. I knew that not all black students were as angry as Donald and Holly and Laura Settle, who had recently emerged as a leader of the African American students. One or two of them had hung around the table during the night of my Ping-Pong marathon, and I realized I hadn't seen them before. They weren't the kids I saw at press conferences.

Pale stuff or not, the faculty was foaming. Faculty member Bill Solomon stopped by my office, in a far less jovial spirit than usual. "I'm going to report to the AAUP that my academic freedom has been violated here," he told me. One of his classes had been visited by Bob Brown, and his authority had been challenged.

"Of course you may if you wish. I certainly wouldn't make any objection to that. The AAUP has been interested in Middleton College for a long time; I'm sure they would be responsive to anything you requested—an investigative team, whatever."

"I think you should call back Bruno Altman from the justice department, too," Bill continued.

"I don't think that would be helpful."

Three days later, early in May, Bruno was back. He had been invited by the mayor and city council (Bill was a council member) to see what could be done about deteriorating town-gown relations. After a daylong campus visit, Bruno made his recommendations to me: the college and community should organize an annual town-gown softball game and publish a monthly newsletter.

I tried to be respectful. "You actually think that would help?" I asked.

"Oh definitely," said Bruno. "And perhaps you could keep in better touch with Dr. Dunbar. I think you might develop a better relationship there that would be very helpful to race relations."

Those are about the stupidest recommendations I've had all year, I thought. "Thank you for your suggestions," I said. When he had gone I pondered his advice about Bryant. We had had a good relationship. What had happened since October, I wondered, since those happy days when we had testified to the state Commission on Human Rights and Bryant had said admiring words to me about my commitment to justice and equality? Maybe I should just ask him. A couple of days later I tried.

"I don't think we've been communicating very well," I began, "especially since you became dean of students."

"I don't know what you're talking about," he said. "Except I know you haven't been treating me like I was dean of all the students. You've been treating me like I was the black dean."

"The what?"

"You know."

"No, I don't know. Could you explain?"

"You know, and so do I. You've got personal stuff with me."

"What does that mean, 'personal stuff'?"

"You know," he said again.

I sighed. "I don't think we're getting anywhere with this discussion," I said after a painful pause.

"I'd like to go now," Bryant said finally.

"Okay."

I was mystified and I was discouraged.

Holly and Donald came to see me not long after. They wanted to talk about commencement.

"We have a petition from all the African American students. They want Donald to speak at commencement."

The college seniors ordinarily voted for the commencement speaker from among themselves, and this year they had selected Joe Cabot.

"We're a minority," Donald emphasized. "We'll never get to have the speaker we want if the choice is always made by majority rule. The African students really want me to speak."

"Bring me your petition," I replied. "Your request sounds reasonable to me, but I need to see the petition before any decision is made. I also need to know, Donald, if you have enough credits to graduate. Only a graduating senior can speak."

Why didn't I ask to see the petition before I expressed my opinion? Because I believed these kids. I believed there was a petition; they just hadn't brought it along. It had not occurred to me that they would tell their friends until they had kept their end of the bargain.

In about a nanosecond, word that Donald would speak at commencement had swept the campus. In a hastily convened meeting, the faculty voted to boycott commencement if he were to speak, and many seniors said they would, too. I convened the cabinet to discuss what we ought to do. I was still waiting to see a petition. Throughout the long meeting, Bryant slumped in his chair and stared at the ceiling. From time to time he said, "There's no peaceful way out." (What? We'll have to shoot our way out of this corral? He was beginning to sound like Donald X.)

We finally decided that this was a matter that could only be decided at the board level: the board would convene in special session to discuss the purpose of graduation and/or restate policy on the purpose of graduation. Rhoda had talked with several of the African American students, and they were of mixed minds. They hadn't signed a petition; indeed, there wasn't a petition until after Holly and Donald had talked to me; they weren't crazy about having Donald speak; he was such a showboat. He embarrassed some of them.

The board made its decision and issued a statement that was to be distributed to everyone on campus: "The board, in special meeting, affirmed the college's policy regarding commencement speakers. The process for selecting speakers was decided several years ago after considerable dialogue." The language was dignified; the meaning was clear: Donald will not speak.

I called Donald and Holly to my office right after the meeting broke up. I read the statement to them.

"You're a liar. You told us Donald could speak," Holly shouted. "You're a liar."

"There's more to the statement," I continued. " 'A forum enabling students to air concerns will be held during the May meeting of the board. Any student speaking as an individual will be granted five minutes, and a student speaking as a representative of a group will be granted ten minutes. All students wishing to speak must advise the president's office in writing at least forty-eight hours before the meeting.' "

"That's stupid," she screamed. "You're a liar."

"I will not get into a yelling exchange," I continued. "This is a college."

"What's that got to do with anything?" she shouted.

I repeated my words and then said, "This meeting is over." I showed them out of my office.

~

The events of late April had been widely regarded as a distress call by the off-campus groups I had first met with in the fall. No organization or institution wanted to be thought indifferent to Middleton College's plight. Sam Powell, the head of the state's legislative black caucus, asked if I would come to the capital and discuss the college and its problems with him. The director and associate director of the state Commission on Human Rights paid a half-day visit to the campus. The administrative aide to Congressman Norbert Ailes, who represented the legislative district in which Middleton is located, spent two hours with me and another two hours walking around the campus, chatting with students and faculty.

Marcella Winthrop, head of the human rights arm of the college's sponsoring denomination, called me a day or two after Bruno's visit.

"The entire commission on human rights of our denomination would like to come to Middleton and meet with you and some African American students. We want to find out more about what's really happening there. We don't like to rely only on newspaper and television accounts."

I tried to sound cordial and hospitable. "I'm looking forward to seeing you again," I said.

The group convened on a Friday morning in the small conference room just off the dining hall. Bryant and I had just had our weekly meeting, the first one since my effort to find out why his behavior had changed since last fall, so we walked over to the meeting together from my office. Our conversation was stilted, but not hostile.

"How do you think the African American students are doing these days?" I asked. "Are they still as angry as they were after our flurry of press conferences last month?"

"Oh I don't think so," Bryant replied. "They've settled down pretty much. They're studying for finals. They're just anxious for the semester to be over."

"How about you?" I continued.

He smiled. The friendly smile I had first seen last fall. Perhaps Bryant had passed through some personal crisis, with his family, with his professionalism, in his efforts to define himself as a black man. I was still willing to consider that possibility.

"I'm doing fine," he answered.

Nearly a dozen people were in the room when we arrived. The only familiar faces were Marcella; Dick Oswald, from the local church; and Holly Washington and Laura Settle. No white students were present. The presiding officer, Reverend Anton Brogan, was African American, and he motioned for me to take the chair at his right. Bryant sat at the opposite end of the square table, next to Holly and Laura. After a round of introductions, Reverend Brogan began.

"Well we appreciate all of you taking time from your busy schedules to meet here. I think we'd like to start by hearing from the president and then from the students and Dr. Dunbar. We'd like to know what the environment is like for African Americans, here at Middleton College, a year after the April Incident." He nodded to me. "Please go ahead."

I read a short, prepared statement. I cited the results of the survey of racial climate—eighty-one percent of faculty, seventy-five percent of students, think it's better than last year. African American students are participating in our strategic-planning process. We have a Multicultural Center; we have African American faculty and administrators now; we have twenty-one multicultural courses that are being taught or will be taught next fall.

Not bad.

Wrong again. Laura plunged in the moment I ended my statement: "This is the most racist place I have ever been, and it has been getting worse, not better. The reason it's getting worse is because of the racist president. She has lied and betrayed us at every turn. She doesn't care that we get death threats, that our cars are spat on, our tires slashed."

"Really!" said Reverend Brogan in a startled voice. "It's that bad? Dr. Dunbar, is this true?"

I held my breath. Suddenly, of course, I knew exactly what he was going to say.

"Yes sir, Reverend Brogan. It's definitely true. I told this group last fall that I was pleased with the progress that the college was making, but I know now that it was all a sham."

Well, I thought, through my anger and indignation, this is a much more interesting meeting than any of the commission members expected. They were on the edge of their chairs. Some rummaged in briefcases and purses looking for pen and paper. They took notes just as fast as they could, none more rapidly than Marcella and Reverend Brogan.

"This is outrageous," I declared, when I could get a word in between the murmurs and accusations. "This is totally false."

Laura's blood was up. "See!" she said. "See what we students have to put up with. She is telling you the same kinds of lies she's told us. Don't be fooled."

Reverend Brogan gave me a rhetorical pat on the knee. "We must hear the students and Dr. Dunbar through. That's what we're here for."

"I thought you were here to get the truth," I blazed. All my anger and indignation and sense of injustice, from blacks, from whites, controlled for months, boiled to the top now. "It is totally inappropriate for the president of this college to be spoken to in this manner and to listen to this nonsense." I rose from my chair and left the room.

"See!" said Laura once more. "See what we have to put up with."

The next day, Reverend Warren Hillis, a white member of the group, sent a two-page letter to everyone on Middleton's Board of Trustees, repeating the students' allegations and expressing his regret and dismay, as a clergyman and citizen, that white racism was out of control at the college.

"You know," said Greg Davidson sympathetically, when he heard about the confrontation, "if you were a man and had left the meeting, it would have been taken as a sign of strength—if the group had even let them talk to you that way."

"I think you're right," I said. My instincts had let me down on that one! I should have smelled trouble before the meeting. I wanted too strongly to believe that whatever had soured Bryant Dunbar on me and on Middleton College had gone away, or at least was something to be kept in the family. We'd soon be back on the same track again, I had told myself. I felt stupid and naive as well as betrayed.

That Sunday I went to church on campus. The topic of Dick Oswald's sermon, announced on the bulletin board outside the church, was "Racism: The Noxious Weed in Middleton's Garden." A timely subject.

The church was more than half full, mostly townspeople, one or two faculty, two or three emeritus faculty. A cast of thousands, by the standards of an ordinary Sunday, and every person white, of course. The sermon was remarkable, and not always easy to follow because Dick had a great many things he wanted to say about his subject. He talked about slavery for a few minutes, and he said it was a bad thing, against God's law. Then for another few minutes he talked about rednecks. He used the term in an appreciative and affectionate way.

"Rednecks deserve understanding, too," he affirmed, "and in some ways they had it worse than slaves in slavery times, because they didn't know they were slaves, didn't know they were being used and misused by the power structure that controlled them." He concluded that the white citizens of Middleton County and the white students of Middleton College were the inheritors of that victimhood.

"They deserve our understanding, too," he affirmed, "for they have suffered greatly."

His congregation rewarded him with a standing ovation. I think I was the only person who remained seated.

~

The spring weather was sublime: warm days, cool nights, soft breezes, and a haze of green everywhere. Lilies of the valley were blossoming in all the shady beds around Foxcroft Hall. It was my favorite scent. The oaks and elms were just beginning to leaf out, to form those cathedral aisles down Main Street to the Edgewood Inn. Piglets galore filled the barnyards I passed each day, and corn planters were busy in the fields until well after dark. I could see their headlights and hear their deep hum.

The new library was finally finished. The dreary piles of slush-soaked building material had been hauled away and replaced with sod. Charlie Fitzgibbon had put the bust of Elihu Tompkins Sloane in his campus golf cart and driven it over to the library. Mr. Sloane, his hard hat removed, was looking stately again, in his custom-made niche. The large redwood planters flanking the front doors were filled with red and white geraniums. A formal dinner dance was planned, honoring the major donors, and then an outdoor dedication ceremony the next day.

I had asked Bryant to suggest a couple of students to speak at the dedication, and he chose one black, one white. The black person was Laura Settle. I smiled approvingly, as though he had chosen Mother Teresa, but in my nightmare vision of the dedication, Laura would overturn the lectern, swing a baseball bat menacingly, and call for the destruction of white people's books and periodicals.

That didn't happen. Laura didn't show up. She hadn't come for the rehearsal because, she said, her parents had come to town unexpectedly and she wanted to spend the time with them. We never learned why she didn't come for the dedication. I asked Bryant later about her absence.

"Maybe she had something she preferred doing," he said indifferently.

"But she was supposed to be here. This was a very important occasion."

"I guess it wasn't important to her," he replied and shrugged.

Phil and Rachel Harkness sat in the second row of the audience during the dedication, under a relentless spring sun. Phil scowled and perspired. He had not forgiven me for firing two of his deans, and he had not forgiven the college for firing him. The library, still unnamed, was his baby, and here he was, only a spectator at the christening. That wasn't my fault, but he probably didn't know that. The dedication committee had decided to leave him off the platform. He was feted and flattered the night before at the dinner-dance, and that, the committee decided, was enough. Even so, his scowl seemed to have become a permanent feature of his face.

Except for that, and for the equally disgruntled group that clustered around Phil and Rachel after the ceremony, the dedication went off splendidly. When it was over, a staff member and I walked back to our offices together.

"Do you know about Donald X's latest activities?" she asked. "He cornered one prospective student and his father in the admissions area and told the prospective not to come to Middleton College. You know, it's so racist, and the faculty is incompetent."

"Oh God. What happened."

"Well, they looked pretty uncomfortable. They left. I don't know whether the kid will apply or not. He wants to play football here. There's more. Donald went to the business office to ask for an emergency loan—no particular reason, just he'd run out of money. You've got to admit the kid's got chutzpah. Whomever he talked to said he thought Donald had a lot of nerve, asking for an emergency loan after trashing the college. Donald considered that a racist remark. Bob Brown has written it up as a racial incident. You'll probably get a copy in a day or so."

A few days later, while writing my final report to the Board of Trustees, I heard screams just outside my office door. Two women, Pat Epson and Laura Settle, were yelling at each other. My secretary was trying to get them to calm down enough to make sense of the conversation.

"This is my college just as much as it is yours," said Laura.

"That doesn't mean you can use anything you want at the college. We've got rules."

"You've got racist rules."

The conflict, it seems, was over photocopying. Could, or could not, Laura Settle use the admissions photocopying machine?

"I told her she could copy one or two pages," said Pat, "but she just kept on and on. She made hundreds of copies. I told her to stop."

"If I was white, she wouldn't have made me stop. I saw her let a white girl use the machine."

"She was one of the student workers," Patty replied, tears of fury and frustration running down her cheeks.

"That's all you know. I saw her copying her term paper," Laura replied, her rage transcending all else.

The warring parties broke up, but the mean-spiritedness of the encounter lingered in my mind. I called Rhoda to see if she had any thoughts about the rising tide of conflict, petty conflict, it seemed to me, with provocations designed to elicit . . . what? She was gone for the day—a family illness, her secretary told me.

She did come into my office the next morning, gravely sad and shaken. "I'm sorry. I had to take a day's leave. My neighbor Leila's boy, he was in one of these prison boot camps—he's nineteen, I guess—he stole a car and was sent there; he got out day before yesterday. I went with Leila to pick him up. It was awful. When he came out of that place, he was running. He just cried and cried and clung to his mother. He cried all day. He could hardly speak. At midnight we took him to an emergency mental health clinic. They gave him something and calmed him down. He's scheduled to see somebody, some therapist, today."

"What happened to him?"

"Leila doesn't know yet. They had some worrisome calls from him, over the months, when he was there. He got into some kind of trouble and ended up in the hospital, and then he got sick. She always felt there was some guard or somebody standing at his elbow whenever he called home. She called the warden or whatever, whoever's in charge, but she never got through to him, to find out what was going on."

"Is he black?" Rhoda lived in a mixed neighborhood in Echo River.

"Yes he is."

"How is he today?"

"Better, I think. I talked to Leila before I came to work."

"Let me know if she decides to seek legal recourse. I know a couple of good civil rights lawyers. You probably do, too, for that matter. Anyway, let me know if I can help." We talked for nearly an hour—about what was going on on campus, and what was likely to go on.

"I'll tell you," she said, "some of the African American students, and I don't mean just the African Caucus, they were crushed when you gave that statement supporting the faculty. They really felt you didn't understand them, and before that they'd thought you really did.

"Then, you know, Donald and Holly and Laura just talked that up—that you'd lied to them, too, and how you lied to them about Donald speaking at commencement—you said it was okay until the white faculty reared up, and then you kowtowed to them. They don't understand about the Board of Trustees. They thought you were the boss.

"Donald and Holly also told everybody you threw them out of your office. Lots of the African American students weren't crazy about having Donald speak—they didn't want to sign a petition. Now it's different, though. They'll sign."

"Just for the record," I said, "I didn't throw them out. They were screaming the same things over and over. I said the meeting was at an end."

"I know, I know. I believe you. You don't throw people out of your office." Her voice grew lighter and she smiled. "Besides, they're younger and stronger than you are; it would be real hard for you to throw them. Even if you wanted to. And I can see how you might."

"So what's going to happen next?"

"I don't know. They're going to do something for commencement, I'm just sure."

"What's the matter with Bryant?"

"Now that's a mystery. There are African American students who love Bryant. They tell me they never would have stayed here except for him," Rhoda said, shaking her head slowly. "But he's an unhappy man. Says he's going to Africa after one more job. Can't stand this racist country anymore."

"I guess I can't do much about his unhappiness," I said. "Let's plan for commencement. It could be a disaster."

~

Commencement weekend, at every college, consists of a long and important series of events. The Board of Trustees must approve the list of graduates (a routine action, but an important one), so most colleges schedule a regular board meeting during that weekend. Many colleges, and Middleton was one of them, invite alumni from certain classes back for the weekend, and awards are given to the most noteworthy. Then there is baccalaureate and, the pièce de résistance, the commencement, the awarding of degrees. The president of the college must be prominently displayed at all these events and ideally should look fresh and happy for every one, even if she is feeling like a crash dummy. When commencement finally comes, the president must engage each graduate as he or she crosses the platform: shake hands with the right, hand over the diploma with the left, and, if possible, make some distinctive word or gesture to each. A certain repetitiousness, of course, creeps into the sequence of presidential good wishes.

We needed to plan well for commencement. I didn't think we needed to fear violence, but disruption was a possibility.

Donald X had announced to everyone that the African Americans would have a separate commencement because they didn't want to participate in the regular one if he wasn't going to speak. It was going to be an African commencement.

I convened a meeting that included Matt, Rhoda, Alice May from development, and Kerry McTavish, the alumni director. I asked Bryant to join us, too. The meeting was essentially about public relations for the commencement weekend—about what Matt called "key messages" that we wanted to get across. One of the key messages, to be delivered to friend and foe alike, was that the college was committed to equality and multiculturalism.

"Could you honestly say that, Bryant," I asked, "because you said the reverse to the ministers the other day." I had to put him on the spot in front of this group.

"I've never said that to the media," he replied uncomfortably.

"Can you support the administration now? That's my question. I need your truthful answer." He looked unhappy. "Because if you can't," I continued, "we need some additional African American voices to speak for the administration, not just yours."

"They can talk to me," said Rhoda.

"I can support the administration," Bryant said.

"Do you think there is going to be a separate commencement?" I asked him.

"I wouldn't know anything about that."

"It's your job to know. Will you find out please? Perhaps Bob Brown knows. He reports to you."

"I'll try." He shrugged, and the meeting continued.

Two days before the commencement board meeting, I reviewed the notes and memos I had collected since last August, so I could finish writing my report to the board. I looked at what I had learned before I took office and in the early weeks of my presidency. Here was a college that had no consistent and clearly communicated guidelines for hiring, promotion, tenure, or pay raises; a college with no job descriptions, with no clearly stated affirmative-action policies or procedures, no policy or procedures for dealing with crisis, no media relations policy or procedure. There had been no clear mechanism for investigating or resolving complaints of sexual discrimination or harassment, or of racial discrimination or harassment. There had been no systematic way of investigating reported criminal, racial, or sexual "incidents."

Now there were policies in place to deal with all these matters. Time would tell whether or not they worked.

A year before, there had been no faculty and no administrators of color except, briefly after the April Incident, a black minister. There had been no services of any kind for minority students, and nothing in the curriculum that would suggest there were civilizations other than Western. Now there were two African American faculty members, four administrators of color, and a Multicultural Center. Thirteen new courses that dealt directly with multicultural issues had been taught this year, and many more courses addressing diversity concerns would be in the curriculum next year.

Students had been admitted to the college who were well below published admissions standards, and the remedial courses they had been placed in had been poorly staffed and taught at little more than a junior-high-school level. Now the Academic Resource Center had been recognized and staffed by people who could truly prepare motivated students for a full program of college-level work.

The jury was still out on Morgan Enrollment Advisors' effort to increase enrollment, but the college had twice as many applications for admission as it had received the year before. We wouldn't know until opening day in August just how many of those applications would be converted into enrolled students.

Not bad. Now if we could just navigate through the commencement weekend.

"Have any students signed up to speak at the Board of Trustees meeting?" I asked my secretary as the forty-eight-hour deadline neared.

"Lots! Every ten-minute period is taken."

"Terrific!"

"Maybe not so terrific. All the kids who have signed up are white."

CHAPTER II

Commencement

The Board of Trustees convened at 10:00 a.m. on Friday in the partly refurbished Alumni Commons. The basics of the library collection had been located there while the new building was being constructed. Although not as elegant as the Founder's Room, and empty but for the tables and chairs set up for the board meeting, the Commons was much more spacious.

More than once, in the Founder's Room, I had felt the oxygen level declining dangerously during long committee reports because the room was so crowded, members sitting elbow to elbow, their backs only a few inches from the wall. When once seated and drawn up to the table, they could hardly change position without the cooperation of their neighbors to the left and right. In fact, I once thought, a trustee could die at the table, his death unnoticed until meeting's end because he was wedged in place upright. The Commons was much more comfortable.

The first two hours of the meeting, when the board was to hear from students, were held in executive session. Trustees only, and the president. None of the vice presidents or deans, and no secretary. The only written record that would remain of the meeting was the list of speakers and the organizations they represented.

The students came, one by one and two by two. Most of

them came to complain about Bryant Dunbar and his failures as dean of students. He was unfair to white students, they said. He did not demand the same performance of the black RAs as of the white. He permitted Donald X to be absent from the residence hall whenever he liked. In fact, no black RA was ever reprimanded for anything. In fact, Dunbar didn't seem to be interested in doing his job at all. He was gone much of the time without explanation, and he repeatedly failed to show up for scheduled appointments.

One student provided a surprising change from this litany of Bryant's failures. He came to tell the board what a great football coach Mr. Lombardino was. He had prepared a packet of clippings for each trustee, including the admiring sports editorials from the (ex-) championship year. He passed them around, repeated his praise, and departed. Whose photocopying machine had he used? I wondered.

After lunch, the regular board meeting began: all vice presidents and deans on deck. Darius Hawthorne, who had succeeded Ernie Newman as chair of the student affairs committee, had no written report to give. Instead, he spoke for forty minutes. He didn't try to answer the question in everyone's mind—why had the African American students declined the invitation to address the board? What he did, I figured out later, was to say what they would have said if they had accepted the invitation. He spoke for them because, for whatever reason, they chose not to speak for themselves.

He repeated every racial incident that had been reported to him and previously reported to me. He repeated the charge that minority students said the president had lied to them, and that she was both a racist and a liar. I felt each accusation like a physical pain.

He rose from his chair and strode back and forth, like a prosecuting attorney, about to interrogate a key witness. Darius was an imposing figure: tall, immaculately groomed, in a well-tailored suit. He was the only trustee who brought a cellular phone into the meeting, and the only one who had a driver/bodyguard waiting outside the door: these characteristics alone gave him a certain aura. He turned to Bryant Dunbar: "Have you felt racism in your staff, Dr. Dunbar?"

"Yes sir."

"Have you felt racism among your administrative colleagues?"

"Yes sir."

And on Darius went. He didn't ask Bryant for examples. He told of the ministers' meeting and Laura Settle's accusations and my abrupt departure from that meeting. He read aloud the letter from Warren Hillis—the White Racism Rampant letter—and then asked, "Who is Warren Hillis?"

"A minister, and a graduate of Middleton College," the chair replied.

Finally Darius sat down, but not before announcing that there would be a separate commencement ceremony and the seniors would wear kente cloths as well as caps and gowns. He would be the speaker.

I tried to sit expressionless through his presentation. It was difficult. I tried to guess how his speech had affected the other members of the board, but it was impossible to tell from their faces or their body language. Men are better than women at looking expressionless and sitting motionless. On this occasion, I couldn't tell even what the women members were thinking. Did one or two look exasperated, or did I project my own feelings onto them?

It was a male trustee who spoke first, on this occasion. John Cambridge was a small, chunky man, a lawyer in his midfifties, I guessed, who had been on the board for many years. He rarely spoke during the meetings, but he was always attentive; his influence was ordinarily felt in subtle ways, on board committees. Now he was angry.

"We cannot allow a separate commencement to take place. This is just too much. If we are going to maintain our self-respect as a board, we must forbid this, and we must go on record as forbidding this." A few heads nodded.

Then, at last, it was my turn. I stood, but I did not pace. I placed my fingertips at the edge of the table and leaned, just a little, toward the trustees.

"My friends," I began, "I beg you not to forbid this. A small group has been goading us for six weeks to provide some provocation that would disrupt the daily operation of the college, and we've resisted. They've called the media here under false pretenses, they've alleged violence where none has occurred, and, some might think, they have tried to provoke violence. They have certainly tried to provoke disruptions of various kinds. Don't succumb to provocation now.

"For particular minority groups to hold separate commencements is something that occurs on many campuses. An American college or university commencement is *very* Western European and *very* medieval. The caps and gowns and hoods, the mace of office, the presidential medallion, the stately processional music, the diploma in Latin. None of this speaks to the experience, or the heritage, of our African American students."

They were easily persuaded.

The rest of the meeting was surprisingly wonderful. I gave the president's report, in which I summed up all that we had accomplished during the year and all that remained for my successor to do. When I finished, I received a standing ovation, led by Darius Hawthorne, who was first on his feet.

Then the chair, Evelyn Hart, presented me with a framed original watercolor of the new library. (Did she know that the artist, a member of the faculty, thought I was the worst thing that ever happened to Middleton College because I had fired his friend Harlan Elliot? No matter. Do not look a gift horse in the mouth.) Then the board passed a unanimous resolution of thanks for my leadership.

At 4:45 p.m. the meeting adjourned. An African American

student was waiting outside the door and handed me an invitation—to give greetings to a rite of passage ceremony that would be conducted on Sunday, at the time of baccalaureate, just before commencement. RSVP by 5:00 p.m.

"Thank you," I said. I glanced at my watch. Minutes to spare. "I accept."

~

Sunday morning, when I drove into Middleton from Jefferson Mills, I felt downright ebullient. It was Mother's Day as well as commencement, and I had already had calls and cards from both my children. This was all going to work out just fine. Saturday, Alumni Day, I had received several telephone calls from parents, wondering if the commencement would be disrupted by disgruntled black students.

"No," I said. "It will not."

"Aren't they having a separate commencement?"

"No, they're having a separate ceremony, before the commencement. Only the president awards diplomas," I concluded grandly. "Anyone who expects to receive a diploma must receive it from me."

More kudos had come my way at the alumni luncheon: I was presented with the Elihu Tompkins Sloane Award for meritorious service to Middleton College. The award came as a complete surprise. Actually, I didn't know that such an award existed until I received it. Since it did, I was delighted to be a recipient, especially since Elihu had been my back-room companion for so many months until he had gone to his permanent resting place in the nameless library.

Another surprise, and a particularly touching one, came from Professor Lynskey in biology: a framed collection of the butterflies of Middleton County. "Just a good-bye present," he told me as he handed it to me. "You once said you liked butterflies."

Indeed I did, and bright live ones were fluttering this commencement morning along the road—cabbage whites, mostly, and a mourning cloak. A monarch, freshly hatched, judging from the unspoiled brightness and perfect contour of its wings, fluttered across Main Street just missing my windshield as I turned into the "President Only" parking space.

African American students were gathering outside the auditorium where their ceremony was to take place. Television cameras lined the sidewalk. Several of the students were resplendent in African costume; all of them wore kente cloths. Laura Settle, fully costumed, looked beautiful, and she smiled confidently into the cameras. Darius was all business: he gave a nod and a quick wave.

When all the students and their parents had gone inside, the cameras tried to follow.

"You can't come in," Bob Brown announced to them. "This is a sacred service. You can't come in."

A considerable amount of pushing and shoving ensued. I entered, hardly noticed. Matt Austin was there, and Rhoda Dillard.

"This is private property," Matt shouted to the reporters. "You cannot come in." The shoving and elbowing continued; the cameras ground on.

"We've got our orders," said one reporter. "Our boss said get pictures of this ceremony."

"And I'm telling you to get out. You have no right to come in here without permission. Who's your boss?" said Matt. "I'll call your boss and tell him what's going on."

"Her."

"What?"

"My boss is a her."

"So is mine," said Matt. Somehow this seemed to defuse the situation.

I slipped into the auditorium. Matt and Rhoda persuaded

the media to wait outside, promising them interviews and ready access once the ceremony was over.

Three chairs were on the stage: one for Bob Brown, one for Bryant Dunbar, and one for Darius Hawthorne. I sat on the aisle in the second row of the audience.

Bob Brown opened the service with a prayer to Allah. He was followed by a young African American woman, who had also been seated in the second row, next to me, who sang "Ave Maria."

Then it was my turn.

"I am grateful for the opportunity to bring a greeting to you on behalf of Middleton College, its board, and its administration. I would like to begin by honoring those in the audience without whom none of our students would be graduating; without whom, in fact, none would even be alive. Today, as you know, is Mother's Day as well as commencement. Would all the mothers in the audience please stand, so we may express our appreciation to you?"

The mothers rose, and a great peal of applause rang through the auditorium.

I uttered a few more remarks—about rites of passage and the right to free expression—and then expressed regret that I must leave in order to participate in another precommencement activity.

I went out a side door to head for baccalaureate at the church across the quad.

"Want a ride?" It was Charlie Fitzgibbon, waiting at the door with his golf cart.

"You bet! Thanks!" And off we went. No reporters or cameras broke the serenity. A nice service, with choir and organ, very peaceful.

Thirty minutes before the scheduled hour of commencement, the separate ceremony was still going on. My anxiety level began to rise. Perhaps there would be trouble after all.

Perhaps the African American students and their parents, or just the students, maybe, would march in and declare the president and all her minions liars, cheats, and racists. My imagination went into overdrive.

Fifteen minutes later, the doors opened from the auditorium, and the graduating seniors hurried along, caps and gowns over their arms, to join their classmates in the processional line outside one of the gymnasiums.

Professor Proctor, one of the faculty marshals, was issuing the time-honored instructions. "There must be nothing on your caps and gowns," she said, "No corsages, no emblems of any kind, and the tassel on your mortarboard must be on the right until after your degree is awarded. Then, at a signal from me, you may all move your tassel to the left side."

Some students always violated these instructions, usually with messages in adhesive tape atop their mortarboards—"Hi Mom," "Will Work for Food"—which were then tilted far back on their heads. This year each African American graduate wore a kente cloth. No one objected.

The platform party came last: the board chair and the president; Joe Cabot, the speaker; Greg Davidson, who would hand each diploma to Bryant Dunbar; and Bryant Dunbar, who would hand each diploma to me, who would hand it to each graduate with a smile and a handshake. I remembered a few commencements of the 1960s: barefoot graduates, shaggy and unkempt, some holding signs with slogans, "Hubert Humphrey Kills Vietnamese Babies." Those days were gone.

Joe gave a fine speech. He thanked his parents for their support; he thanked his professors for their dedication to learning; and he thanked Middleton College for four years of happy memories. "I've made friends here that I will have for life," he said, gazing over his classmates appreciatively.

He was well received. The diploma delivery went off beautifully. Bryant Dunbar looked as if he had never been happier, and several of the African American graduates stepped out of the line to hug him warmly before they took their diploma from me.

Then it was all over. Perfect. It couldn't have been more perfect. Everybody wanted a happy memory, and everybody got one.

As I left the gym, a reporter from one of the Chicago newspapers hurried along beside me.

"Why wasn't Donald X here today?" she asked. "Was he boycotting the ceremony? Were there others who joined him in the boycott?"

"Donald didn't have enough credits to graduate," I said, and continued on to the graduates' reception, an occasion of undiluted joy. Parents and graduates shook my hand, while I smiled compulsively and drank five punch cups of lemonade, one right after the other. I saw Joe Cabot wave to me and make his way through the crowd.

"Excuse me," he said. "I'd really like you to meet my mother and dad." I should have looked for him and for his parents.

"I'd be delighted," I said. "I've been looking forward to meeting them." That was absolutely true. "You must be very proud of your son," I said to them both. "He did a fine job today, and I know he has a bright future ahead of him."

The next day, one of the metropolitan dailies ran a front-page color photograph of the African American graduates, entering the gym. The day after that, the *Jefferson Mills Spectator* ran an op-ed piece written by one of Middleton College's emeritus professors: he commended the black leaders on their theatrical ability—all costumes and posturing, he said. Since they were abusing their opportunities, he concluded, all special services for minority students should be discontinued.

Photocopies of the op-ed piece were placed at each member's seat in the city council chamber in Middleton, and I saw copies posted on bulletin boards at the college.

~

It's hard to exaggerate the sense of relief I felt when every diploma had been awarded, every hand shaken, every parent greeted, every punch cup emptied. Even though my successor wouldn't be coming on board until July 1, and there was much remaining to be done before he arrived, everything seemed manageable now.

The Department of Education had provided a preliminary oral report on its investigation of the Title IX complaint regarding alleged inequalities in men's and women's athletics. The sexual harassment allegations were yet to be reported on.

The federal Office of Civil Rights had issued a proposed "settlement agreement" with respect to alleged violations of Title VI of the Civil Rights Act, and legal counsel was reviewing the proposal.

The state Commission on Human Rights congratulated the college for what had been achieved, and the state intercollegiate athletic association commended Middleton for the way its athletic programs had been conducted this year.

An internal analysis had been conducted of the financial aid office, and new procedures were being put in place that would further assure compliance with federal and state regulations.

An evaluation of the development office had been conducted by CASE (Council for the Advancement and Support of Education), at Alice May's request, and it produced a great many valuable recommendations, some of which were already being implemented.

The Action Team, the strategic-planning group, had laid out some priorities for refurbishing and upgrading residence halls. Funds had been allocated, and renovations would begin as soon as students left the campus.

Task forces I had established in the fall on alcohol policy, college/Greek relations, and judicial processes had all made their reports and recommendations. They'd remain for the guidance of my successor.

Greg Davidson had done wonders in the academic area: new registration and orientation materials, a new catalog that represented what was actually being taught, and draft policies on transfer and credit for "life experience" that meet professional standards. He'd also won the respect and trust of many faculty members who were energized by the prospect of change.

I always took three or four days off, right after commencement. On Monday morning I drove to my cabin in Wisconsin, arriving around lunchtime. I ate sandwiches, drank beer, and sat quietly for several hours on the balcony overlooking a green valley and a meandering stream. Warblers were passing through on their way north; grosbeaks and orioles were nesting in the nearby oaks, as they did every spring, and a pair of bluebirds was examining the birdhouse mounted on top of a fence post across the stream at the edge of my property. Wrens were nesting under the eaves of the cabin.

What could possibly be wrong in the world? I thought fuzzily.

The mood passed by nightfall.

By then disappointments were swimming back into my mind. Why hadn't we made more progress on improving black-white relations at Middleton College? For the press and the public I could boldly talk about "surveys" on race relations, and I could list courses and staffing changes that showed "improvement." I could boast that no one had thrown a punch all year, but what kind of a boast was that? I thought of the words of Phil Jordan, the president of Kenyon College: "Colleges and universities have become the same sort of messy vulgar misbehaving institutions that America is used to."

True enough. Thirty-five years ago they were beacons.

Thirty-five years ago, being against racial discrimination was somehow part of being an educated person.

Thirty-five years ago, a system of racial segregation—de jure in the South, de facto in the North—was deliberately stunting the lives and fortunes of African Americans. Now we were seeing the resegregation of those parts of American life that had been desegregated.

Thirty-five years ago, the doors of colleges and universities were open only a crack to persons of color. Now, things were so much better, weren't they? Those were noble struggles in the 1960s, when small black children took courage in heart and mind and walked the gauntlet of screaming racist rednecks; when young men and women who sought a university education had to thread their way through every court in the land, and then past chanting crowds:

Two, four, six, eight,
We don't want to integrate,
Eight, six, four, two,
We don't want no jigaboo.

When Thurgood Marshall retired from the Supreme Court in 1991, he who had been one of the key lawyers in *Brown* v. *Board of Education*, he was old, sick, and deeply unhappy. At his final press conference, one of the reporters asked, "But aren't things much better for black people now than they were thirty-five years ago?"

Marshall growled, "Things are much better for everybody now than they were thirty-five years ago, but black people are still far behind."

His replacement on the Supreme Court bench, Clarence Thomas, was a finger in the eye of the old warrior. This is the best we can do, a Republican president implied by his nomination, after all the chances we've given you people, Clarence Thomas is the best we can find.

I remembered Charlayne Hunter-Gault's memoir of what it was like to be the first black woman to enter the University of

Georgia, in 1961. After a basketball game that Georgia lost to Georgia Tech, after Hunter-Gault's first day of classes, students marched on her residence. "We got beat by Georgia Tech and we got beat by the niggers" one student was heard to shout as they began throwing rocks at her windows.

The next day the executive secretary to the governor issued a statement: "The students of the university have demonstrated that Georgia youth are possessed with the character and courage not to submit to dictatorship and tyranny."

Some of what had happened at Middleton College in the past months was surely and purely political. In that sense, the skirmishes and press conferences were entirely successful. The administration and the trustees, and especially the president, were so consumed with the African American problem that the injustices and inequalities of other groups were pushed into the shadows.

What about the commission on the status of women? Sorely needed, never established. What about the cruel anonymity forced upon gay and lesbian students, in a macho male athletic culture? Never addressed.

Competition for scarce resources had fueled African American students' claims to be the most discriminated against, the most endangered, the most deserving of those scarce resources.

Our worst failure, though, and the cause of the greatest disappointment, was that black and white students had never sat down to talk together about their respective hopes and fears, and what divided them. Among the most important skills that students can learn is the ability to talk to one another and to listen to one another when they disagree. Could we have taught conflict-resolution skills to our students? Would that have made a difference?

Instead, we experienced a series of "appeals to authority," the legacy perhaps of an institution that had been run from the top down, in a (mostly) benevolently patriarchal fashion, for nearly its entire history. The president should mediate; the president should decide; and if the president doesn't always come down on *my* side, it's not that she is evenhanded, but that she is a liar and cannot be trusted. Well, that's partly a consequence of youth, isn't it?

Perhaps, but it wouldn't matter so much if there were not megaphones and microphones ready to transmit those youthful cries of injustice. The act of transmitting gave them a stature they wouldn't otherwise have had. Was that a good thing, or a bad thing? It all depends.

Before I left Middleton College for good, I held a press conference during which I expressed none of the doubts that came to me in the silence of my little valley.

I began by reading a prepared statement. "I am extremely proud of the changes we have been able to make in one short year," I said. "We have opened doors that had been closed for decades. We didn't always like what we saw behind them, and so we began to rebuild.

"This spring, faculty complained that their academic freedom had been violated, and some African American students and administrators said they were stifled and lied to. We had full measures of foolishness and wisdom on all sides.

"Colleges are supposed to be places where argument and dissent can flourish. Middleton College now is such a place, and I'm pleased that it is.

"I'd be happy to take your questions now."

This was a friendly group. Most of them looked familiar.

"If you were to grade yourself on what you'd accomplished with respect to multiculturalism and race relations, what grade would you give?" the first questioner asked.

That was easy. "An incomplete."

Epilogue

By the time I left Middleton College, it was safe from outside attack, or as safe as any college can ever be. It was complying with the rules and regulations, sacred and profane, that governed colleges like itself. No potential scandals, that I knew of, lurked behind closed doors. There were no more mysterious arrivals and departures, no banned persons, no campus out of control. By the time I left, Middleton was on the way to becoming what students and their parents thought it was when they first came.

Was it also a better place for minority students than it had been when I came? Probably yes, at least for some African American students. Those who participated in planning for the future of the college, who asked questions in class for the first time, and who moved from the margins to the center of campus life received a better education than they had expected when they came to Middleton College. Did that mean that there could be no further racial incidents, no further disorders? Probably no.

To expect such an outcome would be to deny the realities of higher education and American society in this decade. In choosing Middleton College, African American students came to an institution that, despite the promise of its founder, was designed for the Joe Cabots of America, not for themselves.

~

In the two years since I left Middleton College, racial confrontations at colleges and universities have increased. According to the Prejudice Institute at the University of Maryland (formerly known as the National Institute Against Prejudice and Violence), between eight hundred thousand and one million students are victimized annually by acts of what the institute calls "ethnoviolence"—acts intended to do psychological or physical harm to members of racial or ethnic groups, for no other reason than that they are members of those groups.

In response, separatism and black nationalism, tentative experiments on the Middleton College campus, have continued to capture public attention nationwide. Black nationalism and Afrocentrism are presented from university platforms by speakers like Minister Farrakhan and Leonard Jeffries. Their messages are full of hate and indignation and an in-your-face style that seems to match the present mood of America.

The white hostility at Middleton College was most often expressed in snickers and nudges—at African American parents wearing flowery hats, for example, or students wearing kente cloths, or an extroverted young man announcing his quest for identity from a public stage—and in anonymous acts of petty disrespect: leaving obscene or threatening messages on answering machines or spitting on cars owned by black students.

Snickers and nudges? Petty disrespect? Trivial. Compared to lynchings and beatings, or being pursued by police dogs or fire hoses, of course. "Things were blown out of all proportion," I heard again and again at Middleton College, from alumni, neighbors, faculty, students, but never from a black person.

What would have been a proportionate response? I wanted to ask. Because in making that declaration they were presuming to know what was a proper response to particular slights.

"The truth is," Ellis Cose observes in *The Rage of a Privileged Class*, "that the often hurtful and seemingly trivial encounters of daily existence are in the end what most of life is."

Why? Because African Americans have a centuries-long, well-justified suspicion of whites. "Just because we're paranoid," a leader of the American Indian Movement once observed in a remark just as appropriate to blacks, "doesn't mean they're not out to get us." I remember my surprise when an African American woman announced, in a church group in Washington, D.C., that she'd never be an organ donor, because she didn't trust a (probably white) doctor to certify her as dead. Until then it had never occurred to me that agreeing to be a donor—making that little check mark on the back of one's driver's license—was an act of trust.

Again and again, African Americans have been disappointed when they trusted white Americans. At Middleton College, what made the April Incident additionally explosive was that cries of "Nigger!" came from presumed friends, once the battle was joined. Friendship had been less than skin deep.

More personally and more painfully for me and probably for some of them, I lost the trust of African American students, first when I defended the faculty and the college, and next when I didn't honor my promise (as they saw it) to permit Donald X to speak at commencement.

There were many ironies in the Middleton College situation.

When Donald X rose before the television cameras to announce that Middleton College was unworthy of accreditation and that its faculty wasn't competent to teach what it was teaching, he was just about half right. He had seen those allegations documented in the Morgan report. The fact that I had terminated the academic dean in midyear seemed to be circumstantial evidence that the academic program of the college was in dangerous disrepair.

I wanted him and the other African American students to acknowledge that *I* could be trusted to direct the change that would benefit them (and, incidentally, everyone else).

When I defended the faculty and the college, the African American students thought me guilty of bad faith, and worse. Yet as president of the college, my responsibility was to preserve and, if possible, strengthen the college, which was very fragile. Whenever there was a threat of violence or disorder, I feared that the threat alone might be devastating to the college. Even though I knew the college had not treated minorities fairly—for example, recruiting them for football, despite their academic deficiencies, and providing a remedial program that was absolutely substandard—I had to speak up for the college.

I was directing many significant changes at Middleton College, and I was indignant that the African American student leaders used "my" tools and data to discredit the college.

I could not bring about systemic change in a single year, and systemic change was what the college needed. Nor could I alter the recent history of the place: I had to work with the institution pretty much as it was organized, and with the people who were already in place. But I wanted the minority students to give me credit for what I could do, and I wanted them to believe in my goodwill. They did, until the moment came when I had to defend the college and its faculty, when I had to turn down a request from a minority student, when I had to be the president of the whole college, guardian of its past, its present, and (it is hoped) its future.

Every college or university president finds it extremely difficult to know the reality of any given situation, whether good news or bad is being transmitted. Presidents play out the childhood game of "telephone" every day. We know that information changes as it goes from ear to ear, even around a table of equals. It changes even more dramatically as it goes up the administrative ladder, and it changes from its original meaning depending on the interests or intentions of the transmitter. Was a black student's tire slashed or not? Was a black student really run off the road? Was Donald X failing to meet his responsibilities as an RA, or was he being harassed by white RAs?

Paradox. Ambiguity. Bad faith and good. Loyalty and betrayal. They have always swirled around persons in leadership positions, and they have certainly marked college and university leadership in America since the early days of the Republic. "College life was born in revolt," the historian Helen Horowitz points out in her book *Campus Life*. In the early 1800s, students horsewhipped the president of the University of North Carolina, and in the 1820s Yale students bombed a residence hall.

The issues were different at every college, but they definitely were not about race or ethnicity, because student bodies in the early nineteenth century were highly homogeneous, comprising young men of "good" family who came to college to meet others like themselves and to have a good time. In due time, off-campus fraternities became the strongholds of the good-time ethos.

In the nineteenth century, "outsiders" began to seek college educations. Aspiring ministers were the first. Initially they came to the colleges that already existed. Soon, as the westward movement of population continued, their mentors and potential parishioners built dozens of new church-related colleges in the Middle West, so that the preaching of the gospel should not languish.

Middleton College had gone two steps further than most: its founder had promised to educate the ultimate outsiders, women and men of all races. Implied in that promise, however, was that those outsiders would have to adapt to the college, not the other way around. If by mid–twentieth century that meant the black men should play football and the women should be cheerleaders and prizes, who should be surprised?

The natural adversaries of outsiders have been the fraternities, and later the sororities, especially in the Protestant colleges like Middleton, which were once full of rules based on piety and high purpose. Fraternities and sororities have always been places where college rules could be broken. The male culture of the fraternity has also been violent. Although restrictions on hazing are now in place at every college, hardly a year goes by that a student somewhere doesn't die in a hazing episode. Long, thick wooden paddles remain symbols of group loyalty and pride in fraternity houses.

Minority students, the new outsiders, have not been the first to cause campus conflict, and they will surely not be the last. Though the colleges were not made for them, they are gradually remaking the colleges to meet their needs, as outsiders have always done.

There is another way in which history affects our colleges. Everyone is marked by certain historical realities that shape their behavior and their expectations. Administrators and students, parents and children, trustees and professors, were formed by very different historical forces.

The formative historical reality of my parents was the Great Depression. It made them frugal, wary of the economy, and obsessively industrious, well past their time of need. The most important historical realities for me were World War II and the civil rights movement. The lessons I drew were positive and optimistic: America triumphed over evil forces and was rewarded by an era of great prosperity, in which I and my family shared. The civil rights movement as I knew it was high-minded, morally right, and suffused with ideals of equality and justice.

Somehow I never felt disillusioned by what came after—assassinations and official lies, the turn to violence at home and abroad. Disappointed, not disillusioned. An important difference.

The formative historical realities of Middleton parents—those mothers and fathers who called me on the telephone, fearing the worst—were very different from mine. They were adolescents when prosperity and peaceful change had ebbed: when, in 1968, the Chicago police had battered protesters during the Democratic convention, when a dirty war kept escalating, and when college kids were shot down at Kent State and Jackson State, and when riots occurred in dozens of American cities. Their children were probably born around the time of Watergate, a time when both a president and vice president left office in disgrace.

Whether black or white, these parents did not feel, as I did, that these were aberrations in a basically sunny and decent nation. As their children grew up and prepared to enter college, parental misgivings increased, and the misgivings of their children increased. In the 1990s job prospects are poor. In 1992 new college graduates were competing with nearly a million unemployed older college graduates for professional and managerial positions.

Whether black or white, the parents of Middleton students had been affected by the racial events of their lifetime—the riots that took place in dozens of cities in 1968 and in Los Angeles again in 1992; they knew names like Rodney King and Reginald Denny and Yusuf Hawkins. They had watched the Hill-Thomas hearings on television.

Those events affected the way they related to one another, and to the institutions they knew. College parents, like millions of Americans, came of age mistrustful and with lowered expectations. It would take mighty forces to shake them out of their mistrust, and only gentle zephyrs to waft them back into it.

The mass media of communication, especially television, have a mixed record in presenting the grave issues of our time. Because we have grown accustomed to receiving our news in visual form we can process visual information remarkably fast.

Consequently, aggrieved persons try to gain media attention as quickly and forcefully as possible: the young black man in a kente cloth and an African hat, filling a television screen, has told us something about himself that we can absorb with a glance. We may even listen to what he says, at least for twenty seconds or so.

Unfortunately, the media have made cynics of us all. Individuals who use the media, or who respond to it in kind, sacrifice a certain amount of authenticity. Press conferences become theatrical set pieces rather than spontaneous expressions of deeply held grievances. The grievances may well be authentic, but the form into which they have been crafted are not the speakers' own. To a doubting audience, therefore, they are taken less seriously.

They seem not to be speaking from the heart, to be not quite authentic, to be more easily dismissed out of hand, to be smiled at.

When four Middleton College students accepted an invitation to be on the *Sally Jessy Raphael* show, they permitted themselves to be manipulated for her purposes—to hold the attention of her viewers.

All these factors—historical memories, patterns of behavior and expectation, social and economic gloom, the constraints of time and place, the need for television ratings, the sad clichés of racial and ethnic conflict—all these factors will continue to shape the responses that our colleges, and their guardians and gatekeepers, will make to the most urgent issue of our time.

Why then did I not feel gloomy when I reflected upon my experience, and upon the monumental tasks that remained? Was it just my historical "imprinting" of noble deeds and happy endings? I think it was more than that. I think it had to do with a very personal occasion that occurred only a few days before I left.

I had a call from Rhoda Dillard: "John and I would like

you and Bob to come to dinner on Friday. We'd like to say a real good-bye."

The dinner was excellent, and the four of us talked for hours. Not about Middleton College. Not about politics. We talked about our children, and about colleges, and about race, and about being women and men.

Somewhere in the middle of the evening I realized that I hadn't talked easily about race to anyone, all year. I realized, too, that Rhoda was a black person who had entered a white profession, succeeded in it, but never lost her blackness or her pride in being black.

In small ways, she had shared her African American–ness, and she had shared her family. At Christmas she had made sweet-potato pies for several of us at the college, and with each pie she had told the story of its origins—as many Americans do at holiday times. My mother's *krumkake*, my father's pickled herring.

Now, in the soft midsummer evening, we reminisced about the summers of our childhood. "We had family get-togethers at the lake," I began. "Usually over the Fourth of July. That's how you spoke about it in Minnesota," I explained. "You talked about going to the lake, as though there were only one. We went to Little Cormorant, and it was during World War II, when everybody drove old cars because of the war effort, and you never knew which aunt and uncle might not make it to the rendezvous, because the radiator boiled over or the oil pump gave out. And there was food rationing—meat and butter, I think—so everybody saved up food stamps in advance so there'd be enough for a real feast at the reunion." We laughed.

It was Rhoda's turn.

"We had get-togethers like that, too," she said. "We always went to Mississippi, because lots of our relatives were there, especially my daddy's people.

"My mama started getting us ready for the trip weeks in

advance. 'I don't want any smart mouths,' she'd say. 'You-all got to be on your best behavior while we're traveling. And quiet. No whoops and hollers. Because we are going to the South, and it ain't like the North,' she'd say. 'When we cross the Mason-Dixon line, and Daddy stops for gas somewhere, you don't go running into the rest room, because it ain't for you.'

"I always watched for the Mason-Dixon line, but I never saw it." She laughed. "I think I expected it to be like a big white goal line. I knew it had something to do with being white or not being white, and I always knew when we got south of it.

"I loved seeing all my cousins down there in Mississippi, and the trip was always kind of scary and mysterious to me. Like we were doing something brave." She chuckled again.

Her story hung in the air.

"You were," I said. Then, confidently, I concluded, "Things are so much better now."

"Things are so much *different* now," she said, still smiling.

A NOTE ABOUT THE AUTHOR

Gretchen von Loewe Kreuter received her B.A. from Rockford College and her M.A. and Ph.D. from the University of Wisconsin. She has taught American history at Colgate University, the College of St. Catherine, Macalester College, and St. Olaf College. Since 1980 she has served in administrative posts in a number of academic institutions. She is the author of Running the Twin Cities *(1980), and the co-author of* An American Dissenter *(1967). She is co-editor of* Women of Minnesota *(1977) and* The Two-Career Family *(1978).*

A NOTE ABOUT THE TYPE

The text of this book was set in Sabon, a typeface designed by Jan Tschichold (1902–1974), the well-known German typographer. Because it was designed in Frankfurt, Sabon was named for the famous Frankfurt typefounder Jacques Sabon, who died in 1580 while manager of the Egenolff foundry. Based loosely on the original designs of Claude Garamond (c. 1480–1561), Sabon is unique in that it was explicity designed for hot-metal composition on both the Monotype and Linotype machines as well as for film composition.

Composed by Creative Graphics, Inc.
Allentown, Pennsylvania

Printed and bound by Quebecor Printing,
Fairfield, Pennsylvania

Typography and binding design
by Dorothy S. Baker